Relighting the Torch

Andrew Horning

3ʳᵈ Edition

ISBN-13 : 979-8357368430

Front cover art by Hark J. Horning

"In individuals, insanity is rare; but in groups, parties, nations, and epochs it is the rule." — Friedrich Nietzsche, Beyond Good and Evil, 1886

"But, dang it, we can do better than this." — Andrew Horning, 2022

Table of Contents

In Gratitude and Hope

I thank God for granting me a blessed life. I'm married to the woman of my dreams, living in a paradise of natural beauty, with children anybody would be proud to know. I've already lived well. Whatever comes next is just dessert topping. Thank you, God.

But there are, of course, a few things I'd still like to do, so…

I wrote this book to describe how this country was supposed to work, why it never worked that way, what we're doing wrong now, and how we can fix it, so we can leave our kids a world better than how we got it.

This book contains descriptions and definitions of some of our species' habitual problems and deceptions, their relationship to current events and national history, as well as the principles and practices our founders intended, but *never actually enacted*. Also described are some fundamental corruptions of our monetary, military and legal /cultural systems that are literally tearing us apart, both here at home, and worldwide.

The complete texts of the Declaration of Independence and USA Constitution are included, with annotations by the author that have been used by homeschooling classes, and downloaded (and presumably read) by people all over the world.

The book ends with suggestions by both the author, and others, to reshape our society from the bottom, up. As history demonstrates very well, that's the only way to do it.

Introduction

"What a piece of work is a man! How noble in reason, how infinite in faculty! In form and moving how express and admirable! In action how like an angel, in apprehension how like a god!" — Prince Hamlet, in brooding irony

"Let us have a dagger between our teeth, a bomb in our hands and an infinite scorn in our hearts." — Benito Mussolini, 1928 speech, with no irony at all

As a species, we're capable of so many wonderful things! But this book presumes we know the US of A, and most of the world, is a hot mess right now. Ours is a pivotal time of impending global war, monetary/economic failure, extreme social division and …***contempt***. It seems one half of the USA accuses the other half of authoritarianism, racism, greed, terrible Presidents, hate, terrorism, corruption and lies. The other half hurls the same accusations right back. The only thing we all agree on is that *other* people, here and abroad, are wrong. And maybe that's the one thing about which we're all, apparently, correct.

Why *do* We The People, collectively, sustain, let alone tolerate, today's divisive, destructive and obviously corrupt politics? Why do we keep *voting* for it? Why *are* so many of us so divided, fearful and angry when, as a species all around this globe, we've never had it so good in terms of relative safety and physical comforts?

More to the point…how do we turn our collective frown around to pursue happiness, and live together in peace, prosperity, liberty and justice for all?

Do our partisan disputes boil down to a difference in how to achieve those ends? Is ideology really any part of parties? And, crucially, do our Election Day choices actually correlate to what we say we want?

Before I lose you to details and you turn from this book, please allow me three key points and questions:

1. Governments are built on, and depend upon, "conspiracy theories." Which theory will you believe? That we need government to save us from the conspiracies of evil foreigners, pending invaders, rich people, dumb people, and the nefarious race/ religion/ culture *du jour?*
2. Our nation's founders weren't perfect and had big disagreements. But they were smart, better-educated than nearly all politicians today, and had come to mistrust government very much, and for very good, recent causes. So they designed a social organization that put politicians on a leash, and depended on what they hoped was a common morality, yet *self-interest,* in individual people, to serve their *individual* desires for peace, prosperity, security and freedom, by spontaneous order, and healthy mistrust of politicians.
3. They understood that their design was, over time, likely to fail, because that last run-on sentence above was probably asking too much of our species.

The most difficult, painful lesson of my thirty years of advocacy, protests, writing, and political campaigns, is that We The People, really are, admit it or not, despite massive corruption, fraud and deceit, self-governed. We The People, are in charge. We chose our lot. With our taxes, our compliance, our inaction and votes, we chose it, and keep choosing it.

My hope is that this book helps confirm our control, because things won't get better until we realize that not only *do* we have the power to fix this mess, but we also clearly had, and wielded, the power to…

Well…we'll get to that later.

King Solomon was generally correct that, "*What has been will be again, what has been done will be done again; there is nothing new under the sun.*"

On the other hand, our ancient weaknesses of fear and greed, amplified by tribal loyalty and hatred, are now being combined with the fast-evolving technologies of social media, artificial intelligence, facial-recognition, biologic interfacing, surveillance and game-theory for what may be a *new* type and degree of self-oppression.

That really *could*, sadly, make for something new under the sun.

We reasonably worry about AI, and that even well-intentioned and even altruistically-implemented tech could be hacked by the wicked. But the human mind has already and amply proven to be easily hacked. A whole culture can be hacked and redirected to the whims of a nefarious few. One key hope in this book is that we recognize both the hack, and the hackers, and then act accordingly.

But it's wise to keep hopes much higher than expectations.

Things were looking grim when I wrote the first edition of this book in late 2022. Deadly truths about COVID-19-related vaccines, protocols, alternative treatments, prohibitions and mandates were only starting to leak out. China's "Unrestricted Warfare" was chiseling away at us from within. Vladimir Putin's back fell against a Chinese support wall as the USA continued its proxy war against Russia using a corrupt Ukrainian government. USA culture is still more divided and violently hateful than I'd ever imagined likely, and the Biden administration was *arresting political opponents*. We were even channeling Hitler with a snitch-on-your-neighbor *"If You See Something, Say Something®"* public advertising campaign[1]. Markets were flip-flopping like a landed fish. China was buying up both our farmland and our allies, inflation was very predictably out of control, cryptocurrency was in flux as our politicians promised a cashless future. Our governments' genuinely destructive and seemingly desperate political actions were making it look like the biggest wealth transfer in human history was well-underway. All this in the context of a dominating yet minority authoritarian subculture promoting both extreme class-based

---

[1] "If You See Something, Say Something®" is a registered trademark of the New York MTA. But all USA taxpayers are paying for the Department of Homeland Security's promotion of this phrase in creepy advertisements.

hubris, and physically destructive depravity targeting children. It seemed we'd given over our world to Malthusian eugenicist psychopaths bent on global domination.

That's bad. That's Collapse of Civilization terrible, in fact.

And yet, I'm more optimistic than I've been in decades.

Loyalty to the inherently divisive Two-Party System (more on this literally two-faced monster later) is at an all-time low. Until the absurdly polarized and dysfunctional 2024 election, so-called "third party" and independent candidates had been winning elections at an increasing rate. Voter disgust seemed to be increasingly turning into concomitant action.

Unlike previous movements like the Moral Majority, Tea Party – or even AntiFa and BLM, all of which encouraged voters to stay loyal to the status quo parties – voters were *finally* starting to vote *against* the Powers That Be, and *for* what they at least believed to be, *alternatives*. While I know Trump is not the velvet-painting Savior on the Cross his fans think he is, I believe voters are *starting* to see our gaslighting ruling class for what it is. Maybe, just maybe, we are finally ready to wake up, wipe the sleep from our eyes, seek the light of truth, and act on it. That would be *very* good news!

In 2022, the DHS, without any legislation to authorize it, created a "Disinformation Governance Board" headed by a genuinely comical former "Disinformation Fellow" of the Wilson Center. Those who know about the notorious Creel Commission, and Sedition Act of 1918 under that oligarchic racist, Woodrow Wilson, will see some Orwellian irony.

But this "Ministry of Truth" was put on at least temporary pause (or hidden from our view) when, under public outcry and mockery, the Disinformation Governance Board's Executive Director abruptly resigned.

Public pressure did that!

We *can* claw out of this 1984 dystopia to resurrect the libertarian Spirit of 1776… But we must want to. Maybe we need a little help finding the direction. I hope this book will help exhume the best ideas in history, and reignite in our hearts the once globally envied and domestically precious light of freedom.

But REMEMBER…
The bad guys don't quit. We mustn't either. So we must know what we're fighting, and who we're fighting. We're always ruled by a just few mortal humans. They'll eventually be replaced by a different few. "The Masses," often blamed for the world's ills, don't matter nearly as much as those like the man circled below (believed to be August Landmesser).

Don't be like all those other people. Be the one who won't salute Hitler.

Herbert Stein: "If something cannot go on forever, it will stop."

Brief note on corruption:

Whitney Webb's "*One Nation Under Blackmail*" (ISBN-13:9781634243032) exhaustively documents a reality that seems insurmountably, systematically entrenched and evil. You should read it! It's eye-opening, at least. And yet I suggest for reasons of safety, speed and efficacy, we work on our*selves* instead of trying to bring these trans-generationally murderous monsters to justice. We need no more suspicious suicides.

Instead of seeking vengeance, reparation or even fair justice for the past, let's instead open our eyes, realign our system of trust and power, and thus let evil atrophy, while our liberty, justice, peace and prosperity grow.

Even the bad people would like the results. They'll still prosper (with the rest of us), and still have plenty of evil to do in the shadows.

What is Politics? ...What is Government?

"Politics is the art of looking for trouble, finding it whether it exists or not, diagnosing it incorrectly, and applying the wrong remedies." — Sir Ernest John Pickstone Benn, 2nd Baronet[2] (usually misattributed to Groucho Marx)

"But what is government itself but the greatest of all reflections on human nature? If men were angels, no government would be necessary. If angels were to govern men, neither external nor internal controuls on government would be necessary. In framing a government which is to be administered by men over men, the great difficulty lies in this: You must first enable the government to controul the governed; and in the next place, oblige it to controul itself." — James Madison, The Federalist No. 51, February 1788.

It's easy to make jokes about politics. For example, *"What's the difference between politicians and gangsters? Gangsters are better-dressed."* Or an old favorite, *"I don't approve of political jokes... I've seen too many of them*

---

2 Quoted in Henry Powell Spring's, *What is Truth?*, Orange Press, 1944, p. 31

It's harder to define what politics *is*. To define politics in terms of organization, rules, procedures, principles, "…isms" and titles of office always tends to be vague or contradictory. What should be a simple internet search produces markedly different definitions. For example, Wikipedia says, *"Politics (from Greek:* Πολιτικά, *politiká, 'affairs of the cities') is the set of activities that are associated with making decisions in groups, or other forms of power relations among individuals, such as the distribution of resources or status."* This could apply to anything from a playground tussle over a swing set, to a small business startup, to global nuclear war. The simplest dictionary definition from Merriam-Webster, *"…the art or science of government,"* sounds wonderful, but is far from truth. Politics tends to be dangerously corrupt, as well as the opposite of art and science.

So the word "politics," in general conversation, has a very negative connotation for good reasons. Despite our wishes that politics would evolve and improve over time the way technology, art and science do, we're never far from violent regression to our most primitive Follow-The-Alpha authoritarian default. What's odd is that politics is inextricably, almost synonymously linked to "government;" a word with a generally more positive association.

It's relatively easy to generally define "government" as a thing or process that restrains, steers, controls or regulates something. In that sense, a microprocessor can govern industrial machines, a computer, or a self-driving car. A captain can govern his ship; at least until it goes sideways across the Suez Canal, when external force is necessary to govern both that ship back to proper orientation, and restrain others stuck behind it.

So it's best to define "government" simply as force, since force of some kind is what governs anything.

But is that what most of us think of when we use the words "The Government?" Do we think of the deadly force of nuclear missiles and SWAT teams when we want "The Government" to provide free day care, or regulate beautician licensing? Do we think of corrupt, lying politicians who can summon armies, when we ask for more government involvement in healthcare? Aren't politics and government (the way we generally use the words) the same thing? President Franklin Roosevelt made it *sound* as though the two are very different:

"The future lies with those wise political leaders who realize that the great public is interested more in government than in politics." – FDR

What, really, does that lofty blather mean?

Judges often claim they embody an "independent judiciary."

Independent of *what*, exactly?

Isn't the election or appointment of judges one of the most politically contentious, electorally divisive aspects of politics? Isn't the way judges rise through the ranks from local lawyer to Supreme Court Justice at least as political as rising from a local School Board to the office of U.S. President? And isn't everything they do putting law to practice inherently political, and government?

Many people say, "there ought to be a law…" but they "don't want any politics involved." We tend to "want government do to something about…" Yet we "don't trust politicians." But what is politics if it's *not* government? What's human government if it's not politics? Is one an angel and the other a devil? Maybe so.

It's modern fashion to avoid any tincture of personal faith, religion, or whatever we call strong moral beliefs, when discussing politics. But that's absurd because political government is an abstraction – literally a figment of our collective imagination, delegation, and …faith. Our government involves human actors, but has no physical substance itself. Every new law, judgment and civil-movement reshapes it. And by any reasonable definition of "religion," government has become our nation's prevailing one – with such attending revered symbols, idols, supernatural powers, sects, rituals, priests, rewards, apostates, condemnation, and actual hand-on-the-heart pledges of allegiance so solemn, that few prayers to Almighty God are so zealous.

Calling political government a religion is nothing new, of course. And many human rulers claimed to be deities…and at least one still does. And such god-kings, cribbing the Old Testament's 1st Commandment, tolerate no other gods, political, or otherwise. Even in a secular, pragmatic sense, *"No man can serve two masters."*

William Blackstone wrote in his *Commentaries on the Laws of England,* *"That the king can do no wrong, is a necessary and fundamental principle of the English constitution."*

George Orwell wrote, *"A totalitarian state is in effect a theocracy, and its ruling caste, in order to keep its position, has to be thought of as infallible."*

Politicians have not been shy in asserting their religion-of-state. An example from *The Doctrine of Fascism* by Benito Mussolini and Giovanni Gentile (1932): *"Fascism is a religious conception in which man is seen in his immanent relationship with a superior law and with an objective Will that transcends the particular individual and raises him to conscious membership of a spiritual society."* Wow. Who knew?

It would seem ironic[3] that the Italian communist leader and "father of cultural Marxism" Antonio Gramsci[4], a vigorous opponent of Mussolini, had written, *"Socialism is precisely the religion that must overwhelm Christianity."* Gramsci argued that socialism required and involved, *"…an intellectual and moral reformation."*

Then there's the weird supernatural, transgenerational "Mount Paektu bloodline" god-king stories of North Korea's Kim Dynasty, as promoted by the Workers' Party of Korea – like Kim Jong-un discovering a unicorn's home! To be fair, Kim Jong-un did finally concede that Kim Il

---

[3] It's not really ironic since socialism and fascism are only slightly different flavors of authoritarianism. It's more like Chevy versus Ford, or Coke versus Pepsi… except with censorship, prisons and genocide.

[4] Totally un-ironic is that Joseph Buttigieg (father of prominent Democratic Party politician, Pete Buttigieg), wrote most of the translations and commentaries on Gramsci's works in the 1970's.

Sung could not *actually* travel through time by folding space. He did not, however, disclaim the divine familial right to rule Korea forever.

Ironically, some of the most faithful Christians incorrectly interpret Romans 13:1 to mean we must obey our rulers, putting more faith in human politicians like Donald Trump, than in, apparently, the rest of what the Apostle Paul said, and did.

But whatever we *call* government besides, "politics" or, "government," political government is an abstraction that depends upon a preponderance of collective belief, and *obedience*. This is not so different from how we perceive the medieval Catholic Church, or today's Wahhabism. Chinese, North Korean, several African, Central and South American despots notwithstanding, there is no actual person, place or thing that *is* civil government. *It* is an arbitrary and periodically revolving assembly of specially empowered rulers, judges, executives, legislators, and, ever-increasingly in our government, unelected and seemingly unaccountable bureaucrats. George Washington was a flesh and blood mortal human. But *President* Washington was an institution of delegated trust, and delegated force. If it somehow happened that USA citizens were to suddenly and all-at-once stop that delegation – in other words, stop believing in government and acting on its behalf – then the human we'd called President would not disappear. But the actual officeholder abstraction, the POTUS, would, like Tinkerbell if nobody clapped, cease to exist. Similarly, if people turned *en masse* from Catholicism, the Pope would be seen as just another guy. Government exists in action only because it exists first, in our heads…and hearts.

What may be different from most religions today is that government, political or otherwise, *is* force. An excellent quote almost certainly misattributed to Geo. Washington is, *"Government is not reason, it is not eloquence — it is force. Like fire it is a dangerous servant and a fearful master."* The fearsome power of political words will be described later. But political words of even the most draconian law are, by themselves, just words. What makes them powerful are spies and cops and tasers and jails and drones and missiles and cameras and… the litany grows longer every day, and now includes Artificial Intelligence. Every tax, every mandate, every prohibition, every regulation carries the inherent threat of deadly or otherwise overwhelming force. We've all heard that government agents kill people for minor infractions, and sometimes no infractions at all – accidentally, incidentally, or even by policy. And most of us accept that. A common crook can steal and kill. But only government can take your liberty, your home, your family, and your livelihood, as well as your life, property, legacy and reputation. And we bow to that power over us. That is why government itself, more than anything else, needs to be governed. Preferably by clearly-written authority. However…

Force *is* government. When the Sinaloa Cartel shellacked the Mexican "government" in a straight-up military contest[5], many of course asked, ¿Who runs Mexico? But another less-obvious question is: What is the difference between a heavily armed crime ring, and what we'd call "government?" Is it a matter of scale? Armament? Gangsters can be richer, smarter, and certainly better organized than their political analogs (those that aren't themselves gangsters, of course). And the Mafia is more strictly governed by more natural rules, than is the comically chaotic Italian government, for example. Crime rings literally "run government like a business."

Any group of people that gets powerful enough to govern, becomes, QED, "government."

If government can have any "desire" of its own, it's hegemony. The people who run governments tend to want total dominance. They of course want the monopoly on violent force, but also tend to dominate social and economic systems as well. While Christians may say, *"Give unto Caesar what is Caesar's,"* Caesar tends to say everything belongs to Caesar, while of course the whole Bible says everything, including Caesar, belongs to God. While most of today's churches aren't as militarized and political as today's Islam or the past's Catholic Church, it has often been the case throughout history that a society's dominant religion becomes its official

---

[5] In just eight hours on 18 October 2019, the gang trounced a badly out-gunned and out-organized Mexican army to free Ovidio Guzman, son of Joaquin "El Chapo" Guzman.

religion by the force of political government. We certainly see this in the push for One-World Government. Global Domination always seems like a good idea to those who think they know what's best for the rest of us. Just this past spring, 2022, two separate groups met in Switzerland – one for "health" in Geneva, and the other for "economics" in Davos – to push more concentrated global political power onto the World Health Organization. And just a few wealthy, powerful people (like vaccination and "Green Initiatives" demigod, Bill Gates, or defense contractor and AI notable Elon Musk) hold disproportionate, and unelected, power over all.

One of the most intractable and pernicious deceptions in politics is that government *does* things.

No, living creatures do things. Political government is certainly the rationalization we invoke for making people do things. But government, whatever it is, can't even pay for things except by monetary fraud/theft of value (more on this later). Real payment, and all of everything else, comes from living humans. Even "money," however fraudulently and freely issued (an important topic, later), comes ultimately from human action.

Government, being an abstraction, after all, is more *deus ex machina* plot device and bad excuse, than it is an actual thinking, acting entity. When you see road work, or tax assessors, or armed agents kicking in your door, you're looking at real individual humans, with their own motivations and issues.

And politics *doesn't even work!* Whatever excuse we use for nearly all government interventions is, by daily news, debunked. We have out-of-control kings and bureaucrats and armies for two main reasons:

1. Because some of us behave badly.
2. Because we're under the delusion that political force can fix #1.

There *are* other forms of *government* (here meaning, "regulation," "restraint" or "control") *besides politics!* For example, what governs an ecosystem? Is it the plants that harvest energy from the sun? The herbivores that eat those plants? The predators that eat the herbivores? The virus that kills the predator? The bacteria and worms that break it all down into rich soil? …Al Gore? Even the most bombastic rhetoric from a US Senator has no effect on the sun, a hurricane, a virus, or a chicken-thieving raccoon. The interweaving of nature's construction and destruction, killing and birthing, is beautifully, wonderfully, fearfully complex in the big picture. Each dust mite, cloud, killing frost and forest fire has its own smaller, but marvelously orchestrated role in governing a system far more nuanced than our brutish human society. The government inside every cell in the human body is vastly more efficient and beautiful than what takes place on Capitol Hill. In a similar way, free markets are self-governing ecosystems of functional beauty…to whatever degree they're allowed to work. Just as good fences make good neighbors, nature itself provides natural limitations and spontaneous order. Today's comforts and advances do not come from politicians. We should give credit to farmers, engineers, teachers, mechanics, mothers… everybody, in fact, except politicians. More on this later.

Many criticize religious institutions like churches, synagogues and mosques as schemes to control people. There is historical and current global evidence to support this in at least some cases. But aren't political governments inarguably *always* and *inherently* such schemes? Isn't controlling people the whole point of government? Government officials assume supremacy over "the people," and are the schemers of control – always at least tending toward absolute control.

So, "you can't legislate morality" is a foolish saying. Every mandate, prohibition, traffic sign, rule and law is of course intended to legislate morality. Most among us *want* government to control people's behavior to the point that it also changes beliefs and feelings. Some legislation is apparently very effective in modifying what our neighbors think is right and wrong, and what they'll do about it, to all of us.

And while many sneer at the faith that an "invisible friend in the sky" will protect believers, how is that different from the rationale or promise that government will protect its subjects from everything from bad drugs to foreign dictators? Hammurabi's Code promised, "…*to prevent the strong from oppressing the weak.*" What made the *Magna Carta Libertatum* noteworthy (other than that it was almost immediately annulled by all parties, of course) is that it protected churches and noblemen from the King. And of course, what made the Constitution for the United States of America literally revolutionary, is that it builds on the assertions agreed upon on July 4, 1776, in the Declaration of Independence, that "the people" have the power, and duty, to control the power that belongs to, and is comprised of, **We The People**. Yet we've turned from that Spirit of '76 out of fear of everything from Russians to viruses. We The People now pray to government to save us…from even ourselves.

"The excuse we invoke for the evil we do to each other is called 'politics.' Politics isn't just a symptom of our sin; it's an amplification of it. We ought to restrain it. Instead, we rub it like a genie's lamp, pray to it as if it's a vengeful god, and fool ourselves about what we've done and where we're headed." — Andy Horning, 2012 US Senate debate

Through probably all of our civilizations' lowest points in history, and certainly persisting today, is the seductive theory that **the state, or more accurately, the government, should take priority over the individual**, and that individual sacrifices of property, liberty and life are necessary for the benefit of "the masses." That seems logical and even heroic to most of us today, if taken as an isolated concept. The famous tear-jerker in the 1982 Star Trek movie, "The Wrath of Khan" was when Spock said, *"Logic clearly dictates that the needs of the many outweigh the needs of the few."* Poignantly, sadly, as Spock was dying, his friend Captain Kirk replied, *"…Or the one."*

But who determines "the needs of the many?" Can one person like Bill Gates be allowed to make such decisions? He certainly has – from mass-vaccination programs in Africa with horrible consequences, to funding a plan to veil the whole planet's upper atmosphere with reflective particles to block the sun[6].

How many, or few, can we entrust with such power? Are collective needs the same across geography, economy and time? If there are significant differences, wouldn't they make any sort of centralized decision-making

---

[6] For example, the cancelled Stratospheric Controlled Perturbation Experiment (SCoPEx), launched by Harvard University scientists and funded/promoted by Gates, would have sprayed calcium carbonate dust into the stratosphere - theoretically to combat global warming.

counter-productive? Shouldn't our eye always be on an ultimate goal to never sacrifice *anybody?*

On 3 August, 1857, former slave Frederick Douglass gave a speech so brilliant it ought to be a cherished cultural touchstone taught to every high school senior. Here is but a short excerpt from that speech:

"Those who profess to favor freedom and yet deprecate agitation are men who want crops without plowing up the ground; they want rain without thunder and lightning. They want the ocean without the awful roar of its many waters. This struggle may be a moral one, or it may be a physical one, and it may be both moral and physical, but it must be a struggle. Power concedes nothing without a demand. It never did and it never will. Find out just what any people will quietly submit to and you have found out the exact measure of injustice and wrong which will be imposed upon them, and these will continue till they are resisted with either words or blows, or with both. The limits of tyrants are prescribed by the endurance of those whom they oppress."

While it is important to understand what government is and tends to be, it's equally useful to understand what it is not.

Government is NOT a business.   ...At least it *shouldn't* be.

A nation's political system is often described by how it treats the production, allocation and distribution of goods and services, and by its management of scarcity. Economics is, after all, less about money than it is about trust, ownership, and the power of trade. A discussion of the various "...isms" of government and economics will come later. But most differences in isms comes down to who's got authority in commerce, and what force is allowed or denied.

So, imagine if Twitter, Inc., had armed forces and was allowed to use them. Imagine if Pfizer had even one Stealth Bomber, and could use it however it sees fit. Many of us are uncomfortable with the data tracking and snooping by companies like supermarket chains, let alone giants like Amazon, Facebook and Google.

How should we respond when a politician, or more commonly, a voter, says, "...we need to run government *like a business?*"

The intent to make government more accountable to economics and customers is understandable. But an entirely voluntary, democratic Free Market, and government, are opposites. Freedom and government are opposites. The free market, in order to be free, means *free* choices …no *force* allowed. A free market is, by definition, mutually beneficial trade between people without force, fraud or coercion. And government is, no matter what we prefer to think, *force*. In fact, we *want* government to be violent against force, fraud and coercion. We *want* government to enforce contracts and punish crime…with force.

Government is not pleasant words; it is ultimately soldiers and policemen and jails and tanks and tasers and bombs. And these things, while always used against citizens to some degree here in America, are used against lawful civilians more and more every day. Even the US Department of Education has military weapons now. And that is *not* a good thing.

Government, when it chooses to serve its proper role, uses its violence to keep Microsoft from using The Bomb on its competitors. More frequently, however, government becomes the arms dealer and power broker that decides who succeeds and who dies – literally as well as figuratively.

For example, the CIA's Iran-Contra scandal during the Reagan administration, sold crack in black neighborhoods, and weapons to Iran, for off-the-books money to help the Contra rebels overthrow the Marxist Sandinistas in Nicaragua. The CIA, in this case, was quite efficiently "run like a business."

More recently, our government both purchased (with taxpayer money of course) well-over a billion doses of dubiously and still essentially secretly tested mRNA vaccines, while banning and/or restricting alternative treatments for COVID-19. Our politicians deemed some people "essential," and others "non-essential," which destroyed innumerable businesses and opportunities, yet make Big Pharma both villain[7] and

---

[7] Pfizer is a "habitual offender" in bribing physicians and suppressing adverse trial results…as with the mRNA vaccines. In 2009 Pfizer was forced to pay $1.195 billion for false advertising, the largest criminal fine ever imposed in the

unstoppable juggernaut.[8] Our coronavirus fears, and blind faith in public
health officials have allowed government and big business to join forces
for both unprecedented global power, and astounding profit.

People of course become intoxicated, and not-coincidentally extremely
wealthy, with this kind and degree of power. And that's why businesses
of sizeable scale try to at least rent a bit of that power to suppress
competitors and reward themselves. – Or to pay government to stay out
of its business, as Microsoft did in the late 1990's when threatened with
an antitrust suit.

So, ironically, since some of the very biggest businesses lean hard
Democrat, that's why Democrats still tend to blame Big Business for
buying our government. But that's also why Republicans tend to blame
government for *selling* us out. The truth is that it's the dangerous power to
punish enemies and reward friends that both tribes see from a different
perspective.

Polls suggest that most of us fear, and with good reason, the dangers of
"unbridled capitalism." It's true that the proverbial snake oil merchant,
charlatan TV evangelist or vaccine manufacturer could cause us great
bodily and/or financial harm, if even by our own ignorant choice. Worse
still, a perverted physician, an incompetent architect or unscrupulous
scientist could harm us in terrible ways and by means we didn't choose.
This latter happened with the invention and 56-year promotion of
tetraethyl lead in gasoline, known by many from the beginning to cause

---

USA for any matter. Since 2002 the company and its subsidiaries paid ~$3
billion in criminal convictions, civil penalties and jury awards.

[8] Since the 1986 National Childhood Vaccine Injury Act (NCVIA),
pharmaceutical companies have been in a truly unique position of political
privilege. There is no other industry with similar immunity from investigation,
prosecution or accountability.

brain damage and other health and environmental problems.[9]

So it's understandable that we want a force to oppose those who'd contaminate our environment or sell us harmful products. But do we need government to stop us from harming *ourselves?*

The authority and power required to harm people is an order of magnitude less than the power needed to prevent people from harming others. And it takes even more dangerous power to keep people from harming themselves.

For example, it doesn't take any authority to trick someone into buying a lousy product. It takes authority and power as well as monitoring diligence to thwart such activity. But to prevent a person from doing self-harm in their own home, government agents need to spy into intimate personal details. Agents would need to seek out those who'd assist in self-harm; either by contacts, or through a whole supply chain of products and services. For instance, the "war on drugs," by which our government has gained massive power and weaponry in both global and domestic surveillance, as well as militarized police equipment and tactics.

That kind and degree of power has historically proven to be fatal to millions. Such power is both uncontrollable by the saints among us, and too tempting to resist for the worst among us.

That's why we have constitutions, to protect us from the corruption, slavery, genocide and war that politicians tend to promote.

Strongly anti-slave founders like George Mason, with other Antifederalists like "Lion Of Liberty" Patrick Henry were nevertheless slave holders. So these men are no more popular today than is their otherwise libertarian ideology, and there's little point to champion them so long after their death, when it's really their best thoughts that need resurrection. So, while I'm not at all a fan of everything that Thomas Jefferson did, I'll tip

---

[9] Tetraethyl lead additive inventor Thomas Midgley Jr. himself almost died of lead poisoning, yet kept promoting it, and later hit another jackpot when he also created …Freon.

my hat to what he'd said and accomplished with his words about the Rule of Law versus the Rule of Tyrants:

"Our Constitution has accordingly fixed the limits to which, and no further, our confidence may go… In questions of power, then, let no more be heard of confidence in man, but bind him down from mischief by the chains of the Constitution." –Thomas Jefferson: Draft Kentucky Resolutions, 1798.

"Though written constitutions may be violated in moments of passion or delusion, yet they furnish a text to which those who are watchful may again rally and recall the people. They fix, too, for the people the principles of their political creed." –Thomas Jefferson to Joseph Priestley, 1802.

None of the preceding is intended to be the opening volley of an anarchist manifesto. On the contrary, it will hopefully become clear in the following pages that this is a pro-government book. And this isn't a hagiography of our founders – they were all flawed mortals rooted in their time.

But what our nation's founders concluded, and what history underlines and highlights in blood-red, is that what needs governing most, is that unavoidable and typically ungoverned *thing*, we call, *"government."*

"Regulation," and other lies

""Bankers own the earth. Take it away from them, but leave them the power to create money and control credit, and with a flick of a pen they will create enough to buy it back." — Probable misattribution to Josiah Stamp, but it's true enough, dang it.

"Corporate power consolidation is so enormous that even the government could be viewed as a small appendage of a larger corporate organism." — Bryant McGill, *Voice of Reason*.

"We live in an age where corporations are people and employees are not." — Clifford Cohen, *Shots of Wit*

The *theory* of regulation is good. An incorruptible and benevolent power should be able to restrain the bad actions of powerful people and businesses for the common good. The problem is that incorruptible and benevolent power is really not a thing with humans. All power is ultimately for sale or rent, and there are many people ready and eager to buy or rent it.

Most of this book is about restraining the corporate abstraction we *think* of as government. But there's another kind of abstraction that's at least as dangerous, because to many of us fail to see it for what it is, and is not. And because of that, their power and purpose becomes greater, more self-serving, and unaccountably destructive.

So this is obviously about commercial corporations – encompassing all the problems of money and politics.

As discussed in the previous chapter about government, corporations are run by humans, but the corporations themselves are not humans[10]. Corporations can be, in fact, governments…just as organized crime becomes government when it gains enough political and financial power. And as will be discussed in the later chapter "*Socialism, fascism, and other fightin'* words," governments and their corporations can intertwine into one big monstrosity that regards actual living, non-abstract humans as expendable means to the ends of the corporate collective.

Like government, corporations are legal, collective abstractions. They are chartered, regulated, empowered and protected by law for mostly good reasons. Pooling of financial resources/shares, a sort of "immortality" that separates human mortality from the corporation's "lifespan," and limited liability that allows stakeholders to protect their personal property can all be of great benefit to us all, and…the makings of a Brobdingnagian Frankenstein's monster.

That very thing happened with two turnings. First, corporate laws in our nation's early days were almost exclusively on the state level. The federal government got involved only in trans-border disputes, and as matters adjudicated in federal courts, not legislation. But after the USA's Civil War, corporate laws, like just about everything else, became increasingly federalized.

The second event was worse. It happened when the United States bizarrely invoked the cumbersome and still-new 14th Amendment, to foolishly bequeath corporations human rights as "persons," in the **case headnote** of the 1886 Supreme Court case, *Santa Clara County v. Southern Pacific Railroad.* That headnote, written by Chief Justice Morrison R. Waite, greatly expanded into a principle, what was the court's much

---

[10] Bear with me. It's hard to explain this before objections interrupt. It's important.

narrower, actual ruling, on a dispute over wrongful state tax assessment. A problematic precedent in itself, and a good example of how "interpretations" of the constitution have perverted our republic.

While most corporations (mom 'n pops, LLCs, and companies that can't afford a congressman) are still beneficial, "corporate personhood" has meant the difference between some corporations and organized crime is little more than paperwork — and campaign donations made above, instead of under, the table. Corporations are themselves "public-private partnerships," as they rely on government for both their special powers, and whatever restraints are placed upon them. Without exaggeration, they fit a large part of Mussolini's definition of fascism — the bundling together of socialism, nationalism and corporatism. That's a hand-in-glove crony system of political armed force and greed with collectivized risk and "privatized" profit. But it gets worse.

Although ominous government surveillance programs like "Total Information Awareness" had been rightly shelved, they were then "privatized" with CIA funding and technology in the ominous form of, for example, Palantir Technologies Inc, Google and Oracle. Likewise, dystopic DOD programs have been updated by the sci-fi dystopic Anduril Industries and SpaceX, as well as the usual military-industrial complex and scientific-technological elite corporations Eisenhower warned of.

Politically powerful Big Pharma, Big Ag, Big Food and, perhaps most egregiously lately, asset management corporations like Blackrock, State Street and Vanguard, along with a certain foreign government colluding with the "Deep State," have bought out, taken over and stolen, our nation's wealth, health, security and freedom.

Almost all of us understand that our government is corrupt. Most of us see the obvious relationship between campaign donations and their results in governance. Very few of us, however, vote like we know any of that. And so, only a tiny few of us in any way oppose what is the biggest political threat we humans have ever faced — a very quickly unfolding AI-powered dystopia ruled by a universally global network of billionaire technocrats who espouse a Malthusian, eugenicist and transhumanist "dark enlightenment." Many of the "tech bros" ominously refer to creating the "Antichrist," "Mark of the Beast" and even the ancient Golem myth — a man-made slave monster that turns on its makers.

But, "you will own nothing, and be happy."

Our new ruling class is, in other words, howling-at-the-moon crazy.

Unfortunately, most Libertarians and Republicans give corporations a pass as "private enterprise" and "free market" entities, when they are most certainly not. And most Democrats are apparently OK with their favorite politicians running on huge moneybags from their favorite (and politically correct) Big Corporations.

Few noticed that the aforementioned "tech bros," and "PayPal Mafia" were vocal Democrats before they became the most prominent Republican kingmakers. It was fine to most of us, apparently.

But it is not fine. Not fine at all.

Our constitutional design is for a republic where living, breathing, actual mortal humans are free, and commercial operations are, at state and federal levels, subject to regulation.

Unfortunately, the revolving door between regulators and the regulated[11], combined with voters' willingness to elect political puppets on corporate sponsors' strings, is at the heart of both the problems with The Fed/ our monetary crime ring, and Eisenhower's warning against both the "military-industrial complex," and "scientific-technological elite."

We've made quite a monster.

---

[11] The FDA is a remarkable example of this corruption – including that the agency's funding comes largely from Big Pharma.

Constitutional Republic as a Social Design

"Every generation imagines itself to be more intelligent than the one that went before it, and wiser than the one that comes after it." – Possibly George Orwell, but can't find the source

"Hard times create strong men. Strong men create good times. Good times create weak men. And, weak men create hard times." — G. Michael Hopf, *Those Who Remain*, 2016

Many think our nation's founders were not just immoral slaveholders, racist and sexist, but also morons, whose written constitutions were outdated from the start. If there's any truth to that first quote above, then maybe, despite our technological advances and newfangled notions, our nation's founders were wiser than we are today. It doesn't take much imagination to see where we rank against our founders in that second quote – the USA's first century was indeed a hard time, and we've now had generations of exceptionally good times. And it looks like hard times are on our doorstep.

So, before we eliminate the Electoral College, grant even more illegal aliens the power to vote, lower the voting age again, try to push authoritarian socialism and global domination as good ideas, erase our history and even further censor any alternative views, let's humbly consider what those admittedly flawed founders tried to bequeath us as an overall design for society. A design that, by any measure, helped create generations of good times for at least many, that are now, apparently, evaporating. Perhaps we should also review what each of our increasingly "intelligent" and decreasingly wise generations have already dismissed from the founders' intents before we flush the rest.

So this chapter is a brief overview of how our society is *supposed* to work as a *republic* overseen by a *federal*[12] government of limited scope uniting *sovereign states*[13] that each have their own constitutions. …And a few illustrations of how we mucked it up. The generalizations made here will be backed up in following chapters.

REPUBLIC (ri-ˈpə-blik) – from Latin *res publica*, roughly meaning, "public affair." This is a form of government literally of the people, and by the people. There is supposed to be no ruler or ruling class. A republican government is *not* owned by the government. All power starts and ends with the people. Republic, not "democracy," is the form of government we're *supposed* to have in every state in the union.

Unfortunately, the constitution does not define what a republic is, and nearly everyone has it wrong these days. It was assumed at the time of our constitution's writing that at least educated people understood the definitions of rights, torts, crimes, and jurisdictions of natural law, equity and maritime/admiralty law that define a republic. However, it'd take a whole other book to reverse the misinformation that's corrupted our nation for generations. Fortunately, there is such a book: "America's Republican Form of Government" by Kurt St. Angelo. I *highly* recommend it.

Oversimplifying, our founders understood a republic, basing its authority on the consent of the people, has significant authority over legal abstractions created by laws. For example, corporations, unions, and other entities chartered and empowered by contracts and regulated by politicians.

---

[12] "Federal" as in a limited fiduciary, not as we think of the word today. We no longer have an actual federal government, as it has overrun its constitutional limitations to become a *unitary*, or almighty centralized government.

[13] "States" *not* meaning administrative subunits of an almighty power, but sovereign nations of their own. France is such a state. Mexico is such a state. The USA was supposed to be more like the EU than today's monstrosity. This will become clearer later.

However, a republic has no authority over peaceful citizens, and acts against citizens only in cases of tort, crime or disputes. This is why, even by the 18th Amendment, the government outlawed only *"…the manufacture, sale, or transportation of intoxicating liquors…,"* and **not** the purchase or consumption of intoxicating liquors. More on that, later. But in short, in a republic, the government can establish standards and significantly regulate trade and corporate abstractions; but it must **not** interfere with real, living individual humans as long as they're not harming, defrauding or robbing anybody.

A republic is *not* a democracy, or a majority rule where citizens vote on everything…there should be no possibility of voting away minorities' property and life. In a democracy, it takes only 51% to burn it all down. Consider how half of us drive before thinking democracy's a good idea.

Even a *republican* form of government (republican as in *republic*…not the political party that uses the name, obviously), tends to become little better than a protection racket. Theoretically, we pay fees and taxes for:

- Some protection from coercion, force and violence (other than from government, of course).
- Protection and enforcement of contracts.
- Protection of unowned, shared resources (e.g., water, air).
- Conviction and punishment of force, fraud and theft.
- A judicial system to adjudicate disputes as well as oversee conviction and punishment functions (this one's very hard to control).
- A few reasonable, fair, important and universally applied rules.
- A few standards for commerce (e.g., weights, time, measurements).
- Some armed forces as both protection from other governments, and the enforcers domestic government (this is a hard one to control).
- Organizing and training citizen militias (this one's gone since 1903).
- Maintenance of jurisdictions and borders (e.g., private property, gated communities, states, nations).[14]

In both fully authoritarian regimes like North Korea, and wealthy cultures such as ours, many infrastructure needs such as roads, bridges and airports

---

[14] The "open borders" debate falls into the optimistic realm of– borderless, stateless anarchy. Such life would be wonderful indeed if we humans…especially our governments, could behave. There's much to debate, but not here.

are also, to some degree, controlled by politicians. It's common in even poor totalitarian states, like the former USSR, that the force of politics is to some degree channeled to "bread and circus" operations like elite sports. For example, our taxpayers fund professional sports (stadiums, special deals for teams) and school sports for elite athletes even to the point that non-athlete students lose access to healthy physical activity. In some cases, vast government programs provide communications, energy, housing, food, schooling, and even entertainment (e.g., state media and art). Here in the USA, Social Security and Medicare, unfortunately structured as pyramid schemes critically dependent upon population growth, comprise the bulk of our rapidly-ballooning federal promises, spending, and unsustainable debt.

But as the powers and promises of government increase, the autonomy and privacy of citizens necessarily decrease. And that increase in political power, with increasing human dependency on political programs, becomes a monkey trap[15]. Even kept to a minimum, the power to do anything by force and involuntary taxation is inherently dangerous and prone to expansion beyond the original rationale and agreement. And the less-minimal a government's services become, and the more dependent people become on those services, the more catastrophic are the consequences of their inevitable collapse (e.g., Venezuela).

So the design of the state and federal constitutions was to keep inherently dangerous government local, and on a tight leash of accountability – on Election Day and every other day. Voters were supposed to have all the information necessary to make wise choices, and those choices were to be in plain sight. No secrets, no off-menu selections, and *no limitation on options.*

Our founders warned us about political parties and the hostile factions that ensue. They did NOT give us the recent, unconstitutional and embarrassingly corrupt "Two Party System" that appeared mostly since WWII, and especially the 1970's rollout of restricted Primary Elections.

Until 1888, in fact, all votes in the USA were cast as literal write-in ballots. In other words, until 1888, **a voter could pick anybody to run for any**

---

[15] A hole big enough for an empty hand, but not big enough for a hand clutching a treat too precious to let go.

office by simply writing-in a name and office. And until 1888, that was considered a good thing.

But as with all good things, politics just had to jump in. So now, only in 10 states and Washington, D.C., can voters digitally or literally write-in their pick of political candidates for any office. In 32 states, "write-in" candidates must be approved by the state. And in 8 states, writing in a non-officially-balloted candidate is completely prohibited.

Our founders almost universally feared the mob-thinking of democratic processes; particularly the inevitable centralization and expansion of power that would ensue should citizens be deceived by demagogues, or denied information and choices by a ruling elite.

So democratic processes were a sort of failsafe, or defensive mechanism…
…against politicians.

Voting was never about *hiring* politicians. Rulers hire themselves if we let them. Our elections are our means of ***peaceful revolution***, so that we don't have to have the *other* kind of revolution ever again. Our vote is supposed to be a weapon of self-defense, not a poker chip or flag of surrender in a partisan game of odds.

Similarly, the early militia system, as opposed to a permanent professional standing army, was not only seen as the most potent self-defense in every respect, but also a deterrent to foreign war, since *every* voter[16] would have to personally participate in any violence our government desired. Only congress was empowered to declare war, because we could vote away the House reps every two years. Senators were supposed to be appointed by the state legislatures as safeguards for state autonomy, and states controlled the militias until and unless an actual declaration of war was enacted.

This is important. The U.S. Constitution's Article 2, § 2:1: *"The President shall be Commander in Chief . . . of the Militia of the several States,* **when called**

---

[16] Males, anyway. Women weren't expected to be warriors in our past. All adult males were, unless conscientious objectors or otherwise exempted, in their state's militia.

into the actual Service of the United States." And the President and militias were called into that service by **only** a congressional declaration of war. Until and unless that happened, Article 5, § 12 of, for example, the Indiana Constitution[17] applied: "*The Governor shall be commander-in-chief of the armed forces, and may call out such forces, to execute the laws, or to suppress insurrection, or to repel invasion.*"

In this example, the *GOVERNOR* of the state, is the Commander In Chief, until the militias are federalized by a declaration of war…and such a declaration hasn't happened since WWII. This is what the constitutions, federal, and many states, still specify.

The Tennessee Constitution's Article VIII is very clear in how much more democratically controlled the militia system is still supposed to be:

"*Section 1. All militia officers shall be elected by persons subject to military duty, within the bounds of their several companies, battalions, regiments, brigades and divisions, under such rules and regulations as the Legislature may from time to time direct and establish.*

Section 2. The governor shall appoint the adjutant-general and his other staff officers; the major-generals, brigadier-generals, and commanding officers of regiments, shall respectively appoint their staff officers.

Section 3. The Legislature shall pass laws exempting citizens belonging to any sect or denomination of religion, the tenets of which are known to be opposed to the bearing of arms, from attending private and general musters."

So we were to have a **republic** comprised of sovereign states and empowered individuals, not an almighty central, or unitary government restrained only by majority votes, because as John Adams pointed out, "*…democracy never lasts long. It soon wastes, exhausts, and murders itself.*"

The Texas constitution's Article I, § I says it well. "*Texas is a free and independent State, subject only to the Constitution of the United States, and the*

---

[17] Indiana Constitution just as an example. Newer state constitutions, particularly those written just before the Civil War, are much more subservient to D.C. than the older ones, unfortunately.

maintenance of our free institutions and the perpetuity of the Union depend upon the preservation of the right of local self-government, unimpaired to all the States."

But we significantly lost that republic before and after the Civil War, when many state constitutions were amended or newly drafted to transform them into administrative sub-units of Washington, D.C., or even worse:

This is from the Nevada State Constitution: *"But the Paramount Allegiance of every citizen is due to the Federal Government in the exercise of all its Constitutional powers as the same have been or may be* **defined by the Supreme Court** *of the United States; and no power exists in the people of this or any other State of the Federal Union to dissolve their connection therewith or perform any act tending to impair, subvert, or resist the Supreme Authority of the government of the United States. . . . and whensoever any portion of the States, or people thereof attempt to secede from the Federal Union, or forcibly resist the Execution of its laws, the Federal Government may, by warrant of the Constitution, employ armed force in compelling obedience to its Authority."*

That's *not* Patrick Henry talking there.

We formally lost the citizen militias in 1903 with the Dick Act, which repealed the Militia Acts of 1795, permanently and unconstitutionally "federalized," reorganized and renamed the militias. We lost the whole point of bicameral congress[18] in 1913 with the 17th Amendment, taking away state governments' federal representation in D.C. By the 1930s, leaders as diverse as FDR, Prescott Bush, and W. E. B. DuBois heaped praise on the fascist despots of Italy and Germany, and made authoritarian National Socialism, "progressive."

In 1947, the National Security Act created the Central Intelligence Agency, terminated constitutional declarations of war, and overturned most of the founders' strongest protections against corruption and eternal warfare.

Also, around that time and through the 1970s the rapid expansion of

---

[18] The US House of Representatives was to represent The People, and the US Senate was to defend the sovereignty of states from federal encroachment. So, the House was defend people, and the Senate was to defend states against our species' tendency toward centralized oppression.

Primary Elections started legitimizing "Major Political Parties" as only two private clubs — the Democratic and Republican Parties. Why *do* Americans choose from just two people for USA President, yet 50 for Miss America? We even have way more than just two genders now, yet all independent and so-called "Third Party" candidates face increasingly difficult ballot access and election-related rules that don't apply to members of the favored Donkey and Elephant clubs.

It was intended, and is still in the written design, that **VOTERS are to elect the electors of the Electoral College!** (see Amendment XIV:2). And until the 1936 presidential election, at least the name of each presidential elector candidate appeared on state ballots. However, some state code books (Indiana, for example) now *prohibit* the names of the presidential elector candidates from even being listed, let alone being chosen by those who'll have to live with the results of the electors' decisions. Now, while obviously unconstitutional, only political parties, or theoretically, an independent candidate campaign committee, choose each state's electors in processes that vary by state.

> And since each state's number of electors is derived from census numbers, we can see why many want to not only let easily coercible illegal aliens vote, but also count all non-citizens as citizens in the census for the purpose of both more power in the U.S. House of Representatives, **and more electors**; like the almost universally misunderstood "three-fifths" rule that granted slaveholding southern states unfair representation in the union.

Many defenders of the Electoral College claim that its key purpose is to give each state fair standing in presidential elections. But the true purpose is much further from the current collective mindset than even that. Presidential electors were intended to counter the "mob rule" tendency of democratic processes, and temper unwise decisions from the most ultimately powerful, yet fickle and uninformed body politic — average voters.

Electors, particularly what we now call "faithless electors," have the power to veto voters. They can, if faced with a lying, immoral, incompetent, mentally defective and corrupt candidate[19], choose somebody else to save us all from a tragic mistake made by voters.

Half of us are (please don't get mad at the author), below-average in wisdom and knowledge, with many others comprising the other half badly deceived and/or misinformed. So more than half of us are unlikely to make the best choices for the most powerful single person in U.S. government.

Therefore, simple mathematics proves it highly unlikely to get good results from a "Two-Party System."

Judging by our debts, inflation, endless wars, increasingly hostile internecine and tribal divisions, and obviously destructive corruption and espionage, maybe the founders weren't the idiots.

It's good that our young have mostly stopped eating Tide PODS®.[20] We can learn. But at the very least, voters have not been doing what our founders had hoped we'd be doing…using our votes as weapons of peaceful revolution so that we don't have to have the kind of revolution they had.

There *are flaws* in our state and federal constitutions:

- There are no specified remedies for violating them. At least three state constitutions once did specify annulment as a constitutional remedy. But in all cases, these remedies were amended away over the last century or so. Our founders assumed from the text of the federal constitution we'd know that nullification, impeachment, and of course, voting out the bums, were obvious remedies. But we clearly do not know now!
- Seemingly equivocal prohibitions against the "whispering down the lane" or "telephone game" judicial/ legislative/ bureaucratic corruption of our constitutions by incrementally perverted interpretation. While the constitutions' words do clearly say what they say, and it's easy enough to learn exactly what the authors meant, it's obvious that with every new case, every new law, every legal argument, there are new

---

[19] This does not necessarily refer to any recent or current USA Presidents.

[20] Though we still suffer hilariously stupid "challenges" like this.

divergences from core principles and fundamental laws. In some cases, politicians redefined words to better-fit their whims. But the system of corruption has gotten so bad through the past century that instead of consulting the actual words of our constitutions, we now consider previous court decrees, even on inapplicable cases, as the authoritative law. This is of course a violation of the constitutions in both procedure and jurisdiction.

- There is a key principle missing that should at least be stated in every state and federal constitution's Preamble. Ironically, several founding fathers like George Mason and Thomas Jefferson articulated the principle in various ways, but it was only weakly implied in any constitution. The principle was most succinctly and comprehensively-expressed by the DownsizeDC.org people as The Zero Aggression Principle: *"No one should initiate harm against another, or delegate doing so to other people. Harm includes violence and fraud. The key word is initiation. Violence should be defensive only. You must not threaten other people with violence, or ask politicians and bureaucrats to do so on your behalf."* It's also the even more concise Non-Aggression Principle (NAP) and Pledge of the Libertarian Party as written by David Nolan in 1971: *"I hereby certify that I do not believe in or advocate the initiation of force as a means of achieving political or social goals."*

- The valid *purpose* and acceptable *role* of government should be much more clearly delimited. Author's opinion:
    - o No level of government has any authority to initiate force against any citizen except a criminal. Society shall operate on voluntary cooperation and clear understanding of crime versus statutory offense. Crimes have victims. Statutory offenses, where only politicians and their rules are offended, are much less serious (e.g., murder is a crime, while disarming the airbag in your own car is not).
    - o Criminals are only those who initiate aggression (theft, violence), take or harm unowned, shared resources (e.g., air, water) or commit fraud (e.g., sell products known to be dangerous as safe, deceive voters).
    - o Any person, including government officials, initiating force or fraud (this of course includes theft, violence) is subject to punishment by force.

Government *is* force. And over time We The People have asked for political initiation of force for every manner of political intervention. While any sane person would justly denounce the 2014 strangulation of Eric Garner, there's no change to the law that NYC government still claims justified the deadly police action – a prohibition on selling untaxed cigarettes in a city with the highest cigarette taxes in the nation.

There is no apparent limit to the violence citizens expect from government.

So now, politicians assert in court and in practice, that whatever's not specifically *prohibited* from politicians, is within their authority. That is of course opposite of both the specific wording (Tenth Amendment especially) as well as the whole point of constitutions. Constitutions are to restrain politicians, not citizens. So the key principle that really is in the federal constitution, and all the older/better state constitutions is…

> Power not specifically granted politicians in constitutional text is specifically and completely *forbidden.*

The wording of the Indiana Constitution's Article I, Section 25 is very precise, if a bit awkward: *"No law shall be passed, the taking effect of which shall be made to depend upon any authority, except as provided in this Constitution."*

The constitutions, state and federal, as imperfect as they may be, are not about procedural minutiae, or even about laws and regulations. They are fundamentally about authority and trust[21] – who has it, and who does not. Our constitutions (the federal, and *some* state ones, even today) are the practical, and inherently skeptical design for individual freedom, security and prosperity, proven to be better than anything any nation had signed into law before or since.[22] Our current events prove that our founders, however flawed as people, were far more prescient, intelligent and wise, than wrong.

The primary hope of this book is to debunk much of what we've been told, overturn the feeling of helplessness most of us seem to feel, and empower voters with a revolutionary spirit to build our republic anew.

---

[21] Much more on this later. But to be clear, those with the most authority are not to be trusted very much at all.

[22] We probably all think we can make something better. But just try to get more than a few others to agree!

If you can keep it

*"A lady asked Dr. Franklin, 'Well Doctor what have we got, a
republic or a monarchy?' 'A republic,' replied the Doctor, 'if you
can keep it.'"* — From Constitutional Convention delegate James
McHenry's 1787 journal. The lady was the influential Elizabeth
Willing Powel.

"Never let a good crisis go to waste" — Attributed to everybody
from Niccolò Machiavelli and Winston Churchill to Rahm
Emanuel. At this point, what does it matter?

Whether it's from Original Sin or an unlucky twist in our DNA,
nothing lasts with humans; particularly with our cultures. If we
come up with a perfect system, we'll change it. If we arrive at a
perfect set of principles, we'll forget or intentionally abandon them. Even if
we make up our own rules as we go, we'll violate them on the spot. And if
we somehow agree to a pragmatic compromise that's better than anything
anybody else had ever signed into law…well, we've fought against that since
the ink was still wet.

So unfortunately, Mrs. Powel, We The People never actually did the
constitutions as intended. We never extended the constitutional freedoms

we cherished, or the fundamental principle of equality under law, to those we disliked.[23] And the constitution's authors obviously failed to immediately end the states' slavery. So, by empowering a political system to degrade or oppress anybody, our predecessors invalidated the definition and benefits of a "republic" for everybody. So the whole point of constitutional rule of law, ordaining a republican form of civil government, was badly compromised from the start.

But for present purposes let's ignore our government's first shameful centuries of slavery, native genocide/oppression, what happened with Civil War and Jim Crow, also ignoring the expansionism obvious from wars against Mexico and Spain onward, and summarize how we threw away the *other* fundamentals:

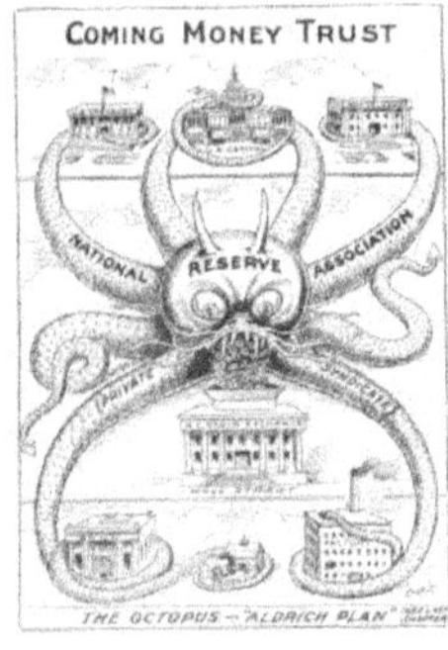

From 1910-1912, we feared occasional interruptions to history's greatest economic expansion, so under Woodrow Wilson's signature, we surrendered our relatively sound (gold, silver and relatively specie-backed[24]) and decentralized monetary – financial system to central banking and fiat currency through a scheme of monetized debt. This was also, not so coincidentally, how we could "pay" off previous wars and prepare for "modern warfare" in the future by... robbing the future. More on this later.

Wilson's domestic oppressions (e.g., Espionage Act of 1917 and the Sedition Act of 1918) to get us into and through the endlessly tragic WWI, and the thuggish Treaty of Versailles, were inexcusable, and set horrible precedents for the future.

Not long after that, our fear of drunkenness led to the prohibition of "...*the manufacture, sale, or transportation of intoxicating liquors.*" While this first prohibition of any sort of trade did not involve prohibiting the *consumption*

---

[23] Of course black people and Native Americans. But also, to at least some degree, Micks, Wops, Chinks, Bohunks, Japs, Papists, Kikes, etc., etc., et cetera...

[24] This is critically important, so it will be discussed at length later.

or purchase of anything, those additional prohibitions came as if by magic –
along with rampant "civil asset forfeiture," police and judicial corruption,
and the presumption that government can prohibit other trade even after
the 18th amendment was repealed by the 21st.

…Oh, and our government intentionally poisoned alcohol supplies, allowed
them to be sold as consumable, and thus killed at least 10,000 people in the
name of "law enforcement."

That first prohibition made for an immensely profitable black-market trade
in alcohol, of course. And that inevitably violent business, and the gangs
that arose to profit from it, rationalized the passage of the National
Firearms Act of 1934; a draconian set of prohibitions and taxes that was
acknowledged to be unconstitutional "but necessary" at the time it was
passed. Of course, it was also acknowledged at the time to have had no
effect on crime. But such power once taken is rarely relinquished.

With WWI's inevitable sequel, WWII, our fear of Germans, Arabs, Italians
and Japanese temporarily distracted us from our hatred/fear of Native
Americans, Negroes and Jews, so FDR took away our gold, rationed and
prohibited a bunch of stuff besides guns and alcohol, raised taxes
dramatically, started "socializing" everything, and imposed lots of laws
against speech, movement, use of some resources and so on. We were
proud of ourselves after WWII…though we did, of course, fear
communists (our allies just moments earlier) after that.

So even more liberties had to be curtailed in that following Cold War, we
were told. One must sacrifice freedom to fight for freedom, we're
told. And past mistakes are often invoked to rationalize today's even bigger
screw-ups. We helped create Nazis and the USSR and all the trouble in the
Middle East, after all.[25] If we don't fund and arm and train our enemies,
who will?

But by the early 1970's we no longer feared alcohol, because we now fear
drugs. So we got Nixon's "War on Drugs," SWAT teams, and a thriving

---

[25] Too broad and deep a subject for this book, but it is important history. A good
place to start is "War Is A Racket," by Smedley Butler. It's easy to find on the
internet.

black market in …drugs. And this time, without amending any constitutions. Police forces grew exponentially in size, armament, and since the 1980's… "qualified immunity" from accountability. Also, by the 80's we feared black markets and drug dealers so much that we got more sting operations, spying, unlimited "civil asset forfeiture" and "No-Knock Raids." This led to vastly more and broader corruption, crime and violence (globally as well), along with loss of individual liberties and privacy, than occurred during the first Prohibition era.

From 1972, when we tied our money to Saudi oil trade, through the 1990's, when some uppity Muslims challenged our petrodollar system, we decided that the Arabs who we'd been manipulating and relocating for a hundred years, then overthrowing and manipulating with our partners, the Saudis, were "terrorists," and so THEY became our biggest fear…for which we've had to sacrifice innumerable freedoms of travel, privacy and finance. Then after 9/11…*Oy vey is mir!*

Now the NSA has replaced Santa Claus as the keeper of lists, and we really don't have any constitutional freedoms at all anymore. We've got only conditional privileges with ever-more conditions on ever-fewer privileges, because, in the absence of constitutional rule of law,[26] there is no longer any agreed limitation on our government's power over us.

Perversely, instead of thanking our nation's founders, constitution's authors and civil rights heroes for the freedoms we've ever enjoyed, we thank soldiers fighting foreigners in foreigners' own homes for our rapidly disappearing freedoms. …By extension thanking the wars that rationalized the loss of freedoms. How can this make any sense at all?

Now we've suffered a pandemic, so we're trying our best to shovel even more power onto global authoritarians and global health bureaucrats when that's now becoming a very hard thing to do. Not to minimize how deadly a pandemic can be, of course. If we really want to live scared, a communicable disease is a fine choice of terror.

---

[26] Quite an accusation, to be sure. But it will be substantiated through this book.

But maybe we should replace our current fear of Putin's Russia with fear of China. China's much more dangerous now that we've given them at least close equivalence in economic, industrial, entertainment, information, engineering and of course military/espionage might. And they've been very cleverly at war with us for decades, and we're losing.

"To fight and conquer one hundred times is not the perfection of attainment, for the supreme art is to subdue the enemy without fighting." – Sun Tzu said it, the Chinese Communist Party has been doing it.

But what we really should fear is that, as China has to an effective degree emulated our industries and market economics, We The People have emulated Chinese brutality, deceit and authoritarianism.
We've thus thrown away our economy, and our freedom.

…And our security.

We've angered much of the world by putting our forces in half the world with the guns pointed at the other half. Our wars never end…even after our President/General Eisenhower warned us about the danger of a military industry. He also in that same speech warned us about a "scientific-technological elite." This is not just the CIA that Eisenhower came to fear, but now Google and Facebook, too, who work in cooperation with our politicians. But it seems we've forgotten all about his sober warnings.

Even worse, all the preceding has rationalized more prohibitions and mandates, more force, and an increasingly adversarial relationship between us and the police. That is a terrible thing.

Bad laws drive away good cops and encourage bad cops. Too many laws mean selective enforcement, which is a major foothold for corruption and racism/tribalism. And corrupt, continuously re-elected, and therefore arrogant and unaccountable politicians, *want* enforcer thugs and the fear they spread. That fear is, more than anything else, what gives politicians power over us.

Our collective fear, ignorance, tribalism and hate is leading us to a very, very, historically, epically bad place. Only politicians thrive on our division, hostility, fear and hatred. They feed and grow more powerful on our discord the way a tick drinks blood.

Our nation's founders would be ashamed at not only the destruction of their gifts to us, but also that we've not come up with any better vision by now. They'd be horrified that we're fighting each other instead of the forces that divide us against each other.

We can't be the Land of The Free if we're not also the Home of The Brave. Have we become the Land of the Serfs and the Home of the Fraidy Pants?

As demonstrated every Election Day, including the next one by all the evidence up to this 2022 election, We The People don't seem to want any regulation of our government at all. We want authoritarian rule and we want it good and hard. That's what our votes say, anyway.

Over 90% of us incessantly re-elect the Powers That Be…and then complain about the consequences. And those consequences have only just started to show…

Hang onto your hats. They may be all that's left after we're done doing to ourselves what we have always feared from others. …Unless, of course, we learn from our mistakes and make better choices – pronto.

So let's not leave this chapter on a sour note. It's critically important to learn some history rarely ever discussed after our very un-civil Civil War. There were some phenomenally good histories and examples we could learn from today, from black citizens. It's sad that their unprecedented gains of wealth and opportunity, literacy, cultural and scientific achievement in those years were overturned, but the lessons and promise are applicable to all of us, and well detailed in a marvelous book published a few months before this one. It's *Black Liberation Through the Marketplace: Hope, Heartbreak, and the Promise of America,*" by Rachel Ferguson and Marcus Witcher, ISBN-13:978-1637583449.

Don't think of it as a de-bunking of "The 1619 Project," because it's much more than that. It's the universally applicable truth about how even the most oppressed people can, when given the freedom to succeed, will do just that.

How laws are supposed to work

"The more corrupt the state, the more numerous the laws." —
Cornelius Tacitus, *The Annals of Imperial Rome*, 109 AD

*"Dying societies accumulate laws like dying men accumulate
remedies."* — Nicolás Gómez Dávila, *Sucesivos Escolios a un
Texto Implícito* (1992)

*"Vices are those acts by which a man harms himself or his
property. Crimes are those acts by which one man harms the
person or property of another. ...For a government to declare a
vice to be a crime, and to punish it as such, is an attempt to
falsify the very nature of things."* — Lysander Spooner, *Vices Are
Not Crimes: A Vindication of Moral Liberty*, 1875

Many state constitutions no longer have a clear "equality under law" statement. As a general rule, the more recent the constitution or its amendments, the less likely it is to reflect our nation's founding dream at all. In fact, all state constitutions have over time reversed the anti-monopolistic, truly free-market (no political favoritism, or tax/law advantages granted to mergers) and have made governments the enablers of corporatism (see fascism in the chapter after next).

Virginia once had one of the best, most restraining state constitutions, but after successive constitutional conventions (especially in 1970), almost all actual protections of individuals against special interests and of course the state itself, were lost. As just a couple of examples, Texas and New Hampshire, in 1972 and 1974 respectively, greatly weakened their previously unequivocal provisions for equality under law by adding special qualifiers:

Texas constitution's Article I, Section 3a: *"Equality under the law shall not be denied or abridged because of sex, race, color, creed, or national origin."* Other state constitutions have almost identical wording (for example, the New Hampshire constitution's Bill Of Rights Art. 2).

That must seem like a fine statement to most modern ears unless we consider how much stronger and more universally applicable the sentence would be if everything after *"…or abridged…"* were deleted. In the absence of any clear limitation on the authority of lawmakers – for example most state constitutions now also lack an equivalent of the federal 10th Amendment – there are literally an infinite number of *"…on account of…"* or *"…because of…"* conditions by which this state could deny or abridge equality of rights. So in the previous Texas example, there are now only five conditions upon which the state could not, in fact, deny or abridge equality of rights.

But isn't this what most of us want? We want special categories, exemptions, provisos and fudging of rules. Most of us want the Other Guy held to the restrictions we think shouldn't apply to us.

We want special rules to either help or suppress, old people, people of color and favored sex/gender whatevers, foreigners from differing places, students versus non-students, certain crimes *du jour*, Democrats versus Republicans against everybody else and each other, and the list grows by the day. That, in working effect, makes laws increasingly complicated, difficult to enforce, and of course unjust.

Laws really *ought* to be:

- Few enough that everybody knows them.
- Simple enough that everybody understands them.
- Important enough that they're applied equally to everybody without exception, proviso, class, looking the other way, selling out/buying off, "interpretation,", etc., etc., et cetera....

The United States Constitution has a fine Preamble. But the preamble is just a preamble. The USA Constitution's first words of actionable law follow immediately after that one-sentence preamble.

The first actionable sentence starts Article I, Section I:

"All legislative Powers herein granted shall be vested in a Congress of the United States, which shall consist of a Senate and House of Representatives."

That one sentence says that only the federal Congress can make federal laws. In the context of the rest of the constitution, it very plainly says that no other person, group or entity whatsoever, can make federal laws. Only the US Congress can make federal laws. Nobody else gets any legislative powers at all.

*"**All legislative Powers**"* are in Congress, and no federal legislative authority exists anywhere else. Not in courts, not in Executive offices, not in bureaucracies, not in the UN. Simple and clear, right?

Apparently not. Because while our busy bee US Congress does write too many laws these days, they account for only a few hundred per year.

Executives, by expansion of the once-reasonable "Executive Order" process by which executives order the details of executing legislation written by legislators, write what amount to at least scores of laws per year in violation of Article I, Section I, and of course they execute them, too. Judges, in very real effect, write and rewrite hundreds of laws per year, and executives almost always choose to execute such rulings as law.

However...

Bureaucrats, minding other people's business from self-empowering and increasingly deadly Executive Agencies[27], write many *thousands* of "federal" regulations per year, or over thirty times as many rules as do the only people authorized to write federal laws at all.

It's *very* bad that unelected, essentially unaccountable bureaucrats write, judge and execute many times as many laws that directly affect citizens, as the three legitimate branches of government all put together.

But that misses the point, which is that ***only congress is supposed to write any federal laws at all!***

There is a reason for that.

Originally, by design, there were two species of congress people:

1. US House Reps were to be and up for rehire…or better yet, firing, every two years. Our founders expected they'd be more numerous per capita than today by far, and that We The People would frequently fire them in favor of new, untainted representation. These numerous and locally-accountable reps, were to be too numerous and temporary to build the fiefdoms and cliques we see today. And this mass of representatives was to have tremendous power; more in most respects than any other part of federal government.

2. US Senators were originally appointed by state legislators to be the representatives of state sovereignty. States, in the original, relevant meaning, would be sovereign governing nations …like Germany and Australia. Senators were to be fewer, and focused on their role to defend state sovereignty and limit the growth of centralized power. That design was killed with the 17th Amendment. And what used to be States are now more like administrative districts. Even so,

---

[27] 103 non-defense agencies (like HHS, EPA, DOE) spend billions on military weaponry and ammunition. There are more heavily-armed non-defense federal bureaucrats than there are US Marines. Even NASA has a SWAT team with armored vehicles, breeching weapons and machine guns. And none get the level of safety and engagement rule training demanded of our other armed forces.

our founders would be horrified that we almost never fire these people.

So, lawmaking was placed entirely into the hands of people who could be fired at regular intervals. And even though instead of just 535 we ought to have a few thousand lawmakers who work mostly locally (more on this later), it's still a tiny number of lawmakers compared to the 3 million bureaucrats in federal agencies who've over time acquired varying and growing degrees of legislative, executive and judicial powers in violation of Article I Section I, Article II Section I, and Article III, Section I.

By what is still constitutional design (the constitution has never been amended to allow what's happening today), bad laws could be easily eliminated or nullified by electing people who'd be humbled and frightened by the eviction of misbehaving congress critters, and thus write only those laws that actually served common interests under constitutional authority.

But damn our foolishness! We've come to believe it when judges say they're all powerful. And we certainly obey the various rules, regulations, laws and decrees excreted by the DHS, BLM, HHS, EPA, FDA, CIA, etc., etc., etc., et cetera…

Why?

Well, because almost nobody ever reads constitutions, or even knows what they're for, for one thing. And because voters are paralyzed in hopelessness, misinformation, and the phenomenon of hopelessness called, "rational ignorance."

Judges say that they and their courts are authorized by tradition, history, legal precedents and "case law" …which can't be civil law because *only legislators can write laws!*

Bureaucrats say they're just doing their jobs…that Congress and Presidents and Judges and the mysterious properties of gravity created their agencies, and that they're just doing their best to fulfill their agency's charter. Most don't even know they're violating our constitutions and everything reasonable. Why? Because, first of all, why would they want limitations on their own power? Secondly, they were hired to do what they do by people who want them doing it. And, such appointees have probably not read the federal constitution either, so they don't even know that *only legislators can write laws!*

Executives claim they have a phone and a pen, and professors, the media and Hollywood Celebrities all go along with such dictatorial powers when Their Tribal Chieftain is in charge. And none of the preceding care that *only legislators can write laws!*

And none of these people could *possibly* read all the generations of federal rules that never go away, and over which they're writing new ones.

With no legal or practical restraints on our government, and innumerable laws that nobody could know and understand, our nation is in actual effect a lawless, ad hoc, authoritarian mess. What we need is a better vision of civil (domestic and global) life than what we're forcing upon each other now. We need to think about who's been doing what to whom, and for what reasons, and think about whether we can sustain this legalistic self-destruction, let alone want to.

We do not have constitutional rule of law. We The People have voted that away. But I'm certain that's more from ignorance than volition. Hence the purpose and hope of this book.

Could we get even a dozen people to agree to a better plan for governing diverse people over a huge nation than what's already ours for the taking? Do we trust our current crop of political cronies to rewrite a new constitution more to their liking?

OK, so let's use what's already the best social covenant ever properly written and passed.

The state and federal constitutions already belong to us. We can invoke them to smash down all this corruption and destruction whenever we're ready. On a single day in November, in fact.

That's not just our power – it's our duty as citizens.

Euphemysticism, and our Problem with *Words*

"Political language is designed to make lies sound truthful and murder respectable." – George Orwell, *Politics and the English Language*, 1946

"How strangely will the Tools of a Tyrant pervert the plain Meaning of Words!" – Samuel Adams, letter to John Pitts, 21 January 1776

"…in the primitive simplicity of their minds they more readily fall victims to the big lie than the small lie, since they themselves often tell small lies in little matters but would be ashamed to resort to large-scale falsehoods. It would never come into their heads to fabricate colossal untruths, and they would not believe that others could have the impudence to distort the truth so infamously…." – Adolf Hitler, *Mein Kampf*, 1924, as translated by James Murphy in 1939.

"What we don't see is that freedom is not a concept in which people can do anything they want, be anything they can be. Freedom is about authority. Freedom is about the willingness of every single human being to cede to lawful authority a great deal of discretion about what you do." – Rudolph Giuliani, Speech on crime, 16 March 1994

It is impossible to overstate the importance of words in politics; hence the hopefully tolerable abundance of quotes in this book meant as a touchstone to historical meaning, abuse of language, and our founders' intents. Words are everything to politics in general; but even more so to the understanding of constitutional design, history, and where we've gone so egregiously wrong.

Between any two people, words are important enough. Words can bring tears of happiness, or pain. How we use words can wound or heal, join with love in matrimony, or divide by anger in divorce. With political government however, words are laws and contracts, judgments and decrees. And those words, combined with government force, can start and (rarely, it seems) end wars. Words can enslave, and words can set free. Words from a tyrant can mean the death of millions at a throw. And these days, even otherwise peaceful, but partisan citizens are intentionally using words as weapons, to shame, discredit or destroy the opposing tribe.

Words can really twist our heads around when politicians stretch their meaning.

For example, the word "welfare" means one thing in relation to a person's or pet's well-being. But it's another thing entirely when it's a government program, or that political corruption called, "corporate welfare." Twisting this one word used twice in the federal constitution has been disastrous in our understanding of the constitution's meaning, and clear purpose:

"We the People of the United States, in Order to form a more perfect Union, establish Justice, insure domestic Tranquility, provide for the common defence, promote the general Welfare, and secure the Blessings of Liberty to ourselves and our Posterity, do ordain and establish this Constitution for the United States of America."

What we've done to the word "justice" lately is tragic, too. That newly transmogrified word has become a rallying cry for the "left" (whatever "left" or "right" means these days). At present it may be hard to imagine renaming a SWAT team a "Domestic Tranquility Committee," or calling armed drones, "Butterflies of Liberty." But if we consider the hotly divided religious fervor summoned by the words, "cops," "Homeland Security," "gender" or even "recession" now, it's not so much of a stretch to seriously consider Orwell's, *"War is Peace / Freedom is Slavery / Ignorance is Strength."*

And *oy vey ist mir* have the words "liberal," "progressive," and "conservative" changed in the last hundred years!

And these words, in tragic particular, have become so twisted, weaponized and used as if magic conjuring spells of unity, division and hate, that before delving into the words of the constitutions, it is important to deal with this linguistic labyrinth.

We'll start with the sensible meaning of "Progressive Liberal."

"Progressive" as in "progress," from the Latin *progressus* – to move forward as opposed to backward; and "liberal" from the Latin *liberalis* – liberty, bountiful, befitting a free man.

People like John Locke described liberalism, like "libertarian" and "liberation," as freedom from political oppression, and as the *individual's* right to life and property; as opposed to the Divine Right of Kings. To USA liberals of even as recently as a century ago, liberalism was advanced through the Rule of Law, which meant that nobody, including the King, was above a uniform, equal application of law. All (meaning all individual humans) were to be treated as equals under law. No special categories or classes whatsoever. No special deals for special people.

We still use liberal that way when speaking of *other* nations. For instance, when China liberalized trade in the 1980's, that word meant their government relaxed its iron grip on trade and allowed both keeping profits and property, and a massive reduction in taxes. When the former Soviet-socialist nations liberalized, they adopted free market and personal rights reforms as well.

That is liberalism, by history, etymology, and all but the most recent, and USA-only use. By any meaningful meaning, liberal is the opposite of authoritarian socialism.[28]

People like Immanuel Kant invoked "Progressivism" as movement away from barbaric authoritarianism, and toward peace and technological progress. Moving forward meant moving away from almighty government and its tribal-drum-beating conformists. Experimentation and progress require freedom – the whole point of regulation and government is, after all, to limit options by force. So "Progressive" and "Liberal" really go together very well in their etymologically proper use.

Modern Libertarian Party or "lowercase" libertarian ideology should therefore be described as *progressive liberal.* That is to say, the opposite of

---

[28] Don't get mad at the author yet. Wait until the next chapter.

what those words mean in popular use today. So, the newer phrase, "classical liberal," is akin to saying "classical facts" are actual facts, while today's "facts" are lies.

The various authoritarian "isms" are detailed in the next chapter. But in short, today's Marxists and "Democratic Socialists" are literally the opposite of the preceding definition of liberal. Of course, it's understandable why anybody would want to call themselves a progressive liberal by the "classical liberal" definition. Who wouldn't?

"Conservatives" wouldn't, of course, as "liberal" is a condemnation to them.

Yet political "conservatives" had for centuries rejected notions of classless individualism and egalitarianism, and instead promoted hierarchy under a distinct ruling class; typically hereditary at that. Such caste-based kings, rulers, Shahs and Caesars have been the human societal default, after all. Conservatives defended such elitist schemes against the common rabble since well before the word "conservative" was uttered. To simplify a bit, conservatism is the conservation of our most basic animal default of Follow-The-Alpha authoritarian rule. More like a wolf pack than the more elegant image of kingly robe and scepter we'd likely prefer.

So, today? We have at least a few, limited hereditary political dynasties (e.g., Kennedy, Bush, Obama). We definitely have a ruling class we've empowered over almost every physical aspect of our lives. We have no "rights" our rulers cannot seize for any number of political whims. "The Patriot Act," and other similar euphemysticism, is all about gutting the rule of law and everything our founders, as well as thinkers like Locke and Kant, were all about. With something cynically deemed, "historic" every day now (literally historic, as in regressing to pre-Hammurabic barbarism), we've become lock-stepping, militarized, silence-the-opposition, book-burning fascists.

That word "fascist" isn't invoked without cause. By the way Mussolini defined his corporatist, nationalist variation of socialism, the USA is and has been for some time, and to an embarrassing degree, fascist. FDR admired Benito Mussolini, calling him *the admirable Italian gentlemen*," and

Mussolini in turn said he was flattered that FDR's "New Deal" so closely mirrored Il Duce's "Third Way" that Mussolini called the New Deal "fascism."

Hitler, interviewed for the July 10, 1933 New York Times said, "*I have sympathy with President Roosevelt because he marches straight to his objective over Congress, over lobbies, over stubborn bureaucracies.*"

In other words, two of history's most reviled men expressed admiration of FDR…who at least initially admired them right back to the point of copying their rhetoric and policies now called "liberal."

Since Republicans like Teddy Roosevelt started a "Progressive Movement" in the USA, "Progressive Liberal" in modern parlance has become more authentically, "regressive conservatism," if nobody's already polluted that phrase.

In other words, our use of those tribal labels has almost completely flipped. "Almost" because conservatism now means close to the same thing as it did before; which is to say it means pretty much the same thing as progressive liberal does today: Politicians are in charge, and we're not.

In other-other words, what we now call "liberal," "progressive," "conservative," "Democratic" or "Republican" all means two wings on the same bird: stone-age authoritarianism, self-aggrandizing tribalism marketed to divide and oppose tribes. The opposition of the various incorporated factions are based upon false dichotomies that work very well to manipulate y'all[29] and distract us from the massive corruption that's lining the rulers' pockets and consolidating their power.

Perhaps the most devilishly clever and destructive word contortion is the common equation of "government," with, "public." "Public school" sounds much better than "political school," though the latter has become the most accurate label today.

It is this kind and degree of linguistic and cultural distortion that

---

[29] "Y'all," "all y'all" "all you" and "yous" are clear and appropriate second-person plural pronouns that carry their own regional, class and tribal associations.

necessitates the following chapter.

Socialism, fascism, and other fightin' words

"There is no difference between communism and socialism, except in the means of achieving the same ultimate end: communism proposes to enslave men by force, socialism - by vote. It is merely the difference between murder and suicide." — Ayn Rand, *"The Ayn Rand Lexicon: Objectivism from A to Z,"* 1988

"If Fascism Ever Comes to America, It Will Come in the Name of Liberalism" — Ronald Reagan, "60 Minutes" interview, 1975

"There are more true believers in Marxism at the University of California in Berkeley than in the whole communist Czechoslovakia" — Vaclav Klaus, speaking at EFDD conference, *"Europe 25 Years After the Fall of the Iron Curtain,"* 2014.

It is unfortunately necessary to address some words that have wildly variable meaning today – words that cloud our understanding of political reality, and each other – turning discussion into angry harangues, or silence. It's unfortunate that we have so many categories of authoritarianism (socialism, fascism, communism…) that each has its own jealously defended "…ism" and tribal pride; while so little room is allowed for alternative views. Also unfortunate is that what follows is nearly opposite what our children have been taught in schools, and what we've been told by mainstream media through the past few decades.

First, "fascism." If you look up the definition today, you'll see one of today's most popular denunciations – "Far Right," sometimes with a picture of Hitler. But fascism was born in Italy from socialist, union and farmers' groups from the Italian word, "*fasci*," meaning, "bundles." Former socialist writer Mussolini invoked his fascism as the bundling of socialism, with nationalism and corporatism. Corporatism, in this case, was what we'd call "Crony capitalism," or a hand-in-glove relationship between rulers and wealthy businessmen. The NSDAP *Nationalsozialistische Deutsche Arbeiters Partei*, or National Socialist German Workers' Party (Nazis) claimed to be an anti-capitalist, socialist party. Hitler wrote of his own economic plan, "*Point No. 13 in that program demands the nationalization of all public companies, in other words socialization, or what is known here as socialism.*" On the other hand, Hitler did, like Mussolini, allow for private property ownership: "*Socialism, unlike Marxism, does not repudiate private property.*"

The distinctions between Mussolini's fascism, Hitler's nationalist socialism (as opposed to what Hitler called "Jewish Marxism"), Stalin and Mao's socialism and communism, did involve varying concepts of race and nation, with socialism/communism being globalist, as opposed to nationalist. And today's market-focused and obviously nationalist and racist China much more closely resembles Mussolini's fascism, or Hitler' s Nazism, than Marx's socialism. But all are *authoritarians* who stifled dissent, and killed by the millions and scores of millions…of their own people. Yet somehow only "fascism" carries the universally negative connotation today.

So let's move on to the classical definitions of socialism, as opposed to what's commonly in print now:

- Socialism is **not** "communal," "social" or actual "public" control of property and ownership of the means of production. It is government control of all the above. That means politicians control property …not us. Politicians own the means of production…we don't. When the Venezuelan government took over the oil industry; it did *not* hand it over to the Venezuelan people in a joint-ownership scheme. Yet self-described socialists the world over hailed the Venezuelan Model as "real socialism," until it failed badly.
- "Social programs" are themselves not socialist. There are many market economies where extensive social programs like "safety nets" and

infrastructure, along with private property and privately-owned business coexist – Scandinavian countries being obvious examples.

- Some definitions include the elimination of private property, but this overlaps with communism, and contradicts Marx's admittedly self-contradictory definitions. And only the most rabidly zealous cellphone and home ownership-eschewing leftists would want this to be part of the definition. But there are certainly no real property *rights* under socialism. Politicians may take whatever you have whenever they want to. Just like our government today, with "eminent domain" takings and other mandates.

- Classless society. This would be wonderful. It is very much the opposite of what happens anywhere on the planet today, but it sure would be nice. Unfortunately, socialist nations mutate "classless" into the singular class of The Party, where the ruling class wears matching outfits and purges all opposition (see USSR, China, North Korea, Khmer Rouge Cambodia). And today's self-appointed "liberals" are all about special classes and special rules for special people – the absolute opposite of classless. Everybody gets a societal cubbyhole.

- In Marxist theory, an intermediary/transitional form of government between capitalism and communism distinguished by unequal distribution of property and income. *"Corresponding to this is also a political transition period in which the state can be nothing but the revolutionary dictatorship of the proletariat."* – Karl Marx

Socialism

From Wikipedia, the free encyclopedia

For other uses, see Socialism (disambiguation).

Socialism is a range of economic and social systems characterised by social ownership and democratic control of the means of production,[10] as well as the political theories, and movements associated with them.[11] Social ownership may refer to forms of public, collective, or cooperative ownership, or to citizen ownership of equity.[12] There are many varieties of socialism and there is no single definition encapsulating all of them.[13] Social ownership is the common element shared by its various forms.[5][14][15]

The use and public, common intention of the word "socialism" has changed a LOT recently (see Wikipedia's 2018 definition, above[30], for

---

[30] OK, I confess that I added to the graphics.

example). So let's contrast it to communism, as defined by Marx:

- The state is eliminated (true anarchy) and all property and means of production is owned equally by the people as a collective. This has existed from time to time throughout history. In the USA there were the briefly successful Shaker and Oneida communes, among many others, that our government ignored. There are so-called "communes" today, and they do share property and production as a collective to some degree. But they are certainly not free of political governance (nothing is!), and are therefore not communist by Marx's definition.
- No private property. *"The theory of Communism may be summed up in one sentence: Abolish all private property."* – Karl Marx. This is much harder to sustain, but in small groups of shared beliefs, it does still happen that people shed personal ownership and privacy for the commune's benefit. This can work, though only briefly, even with the "Two Kinds of People" discussed in the next chapter. There is, however, a strong positive correlation between private property ownership and success of the community. In other words, it is to the benefit of the whole for individuals to own things and build personal wealth from the fruits of their motivated labor.
- Distribution of goods and services by: *"From each according to his abilities, to each according to his needs."* – Karl Marx. As above, this can happen, if only briefly. Some seem to like it. And if they don't force it on others, then more power to them.
- Classless society, as previous. What a wonderful dream!

One of socialists' key critiques of free markets and capitalism is that unregulated trade becomes, in the words of Karl Marx's *Das Kapital*, a *"...process in the accumulation and concentration of capital, and expresses itself finally as a centralization of already existing capitals in a few hands and a decapitalization of many."*

This is a true tendency of any system, not just capitalism – see the ruling class of Venezuela, North Korea, Cuba...or even the most "successful" authoritarian state that calls itself communist – China. Powerful people become enormously wealthy, while the politically unfavored folk get dissected for body parts. So Marx wasn't totally wrong, since it's just human nature and the history of any governing system that some people get richer than others, *particularly* where injustice is enforced and sustained by…government!

Marx proposed socialism as a violent takeover and intermediate step to forcefully-imposed, but thereafter theoretically peaceful, communism. And it's useful to consider communism an endpoint of anarchy, since the social arrangement could, theoretically, be achieved by either peaceful libertarian or violent authoritarian means. And that endpoint is to get to the same politician-free, self-governing society. …Who wouldn't like that? Well, apparently humans wouldn't like that. It takes only a few to make a king for everybody.

Words change all the time. The English language hardly resembles what it did before the Vikings, Francophiles and Shakespeare started messing with it. Marx himself redefined what the earlier New Harmony, Indiana "Owenite" socialists called, "socialism."

There are obviously many decent, well-meaning, well-educated and very intelligent socialists. But most seem to perform the same, subtle, self-deluding linguistic alchemy:

They trans-substantiate politicians/rulers into "The People," the way Catholics turn wine into Christ's blood. They are, in their clearer moments, advocating communism without the bloodshed necessary to separate people from their rights and property. Outside of the small communes that exist independent of government, the dreams of communist felicity, equality and peace invariably arrive in the person of a uniformed despot. And as with "Communist" (certainly not stateless or classless!) China today, it is typically a despot who tolerates no other religion but The State.

In other words, today's socialists dismiss the inevitably corrupt, violent and impoverishing despotism of an almighty government, and transmute the realities of authoritarianism (yes, socialism *is* authoritarianism) into oddly-detached dreams of a pseudo-Marxian Kumbaya.

Now, to a degree and in a way, we all do something like that. We like to imagine a perfect future and don't fuss the details in how to get there. That's a problem that misinformation and divisive, tribal communication makes worse.

All government *is* by at least by resigned or ignorant consent of the governed majority. Politicians, elites and even the legions of bureaucrats all put-together, are vastly outnumbered by the people who in one way or another, tolerate being ruled. So even the most oppressive tyrants reflect The People's willingness to submit, if nothing else. Governments reflect the people who empower the abstractions of state.

But today's socialists aren't thinking of We The People as a republic with representative politicians. They see their chosen politicians as comrades fighting for The People, and yet they're also elitists who see The People as untrustworthy others, in need of ever-more restriction, prohibitions, mandates and, ominously, silencing. Even more strangely, as they're asking politicians to take over every aspect of our lives, they're proposing this will lead to freedom.

Wouldn't this rationale for violence appeal to modern socialists' ears? "*We call communism the real movement which abolishes the present state of things. … the alteration of men on a mass scale is, necessary, … a revolution; this revolution is necessary, therefore, not only because the ruling class cannot be overthrown in any other way, but also because the class overthrowing it can only in a revolution succeed in ridding itself of all the muck of ages and become fitted to found society anew.*" – Karl Marx[31]

And how about this one: "*Let the ruling classes tremble at a communist revolution. The proletarians have nothing to lose but their chains. They have a world to win. Workingmen of all countries, unite!*" – Karl Marx

And this one from Marx is always true: "*A nation cannot become free and at the same time continue to oppress other nations.*"

But now let's consider the label "Democratic Socialist" (which is itself very Marxian: "*Democracy is the road to socialism*").

Problem #1 – Democracy is majority rule. Majority as opposed to any minority.   A less-appealing name for it is "mob rule." The saying, "*Democracy is two wolves and a lamb voting on what to have for lunch. Liberty is a well-armed lamb contesting the vote*" is misattributed to Benjamin Franklin, but it's accurate. In at least rhetoric, most self-described "Democratic

---

[31] To be clear, ellipses (…) in quotes indicate removal of some text, or in the case of Marx, needless and contradictory verbosity.

Socialists" wouldn't promote actual democracy. They couldn't, and still claim any concern for minorities or disdain of lynch mobs. Democratic socialists' claim to be the champions of the downtrodden and minorities is thus a non-sequitur.

Problem #2 – We may not admit that we have what we vote for, but unless all of our elections are a fraud (and let's not rule anything out[32]), then we already have what the majority have chosen. We may claim a single-digit-approval rate of our congress, but those politicians enjoy a ~90% reelection rate every Election Day. So is there an endpoint? When will this New Deal finally be perfected by our democratic processes? And why do opposing voices need to be suppressed and/or arrested if we're submitting to the will of the majority and the beauty of Truth?

Problem #3 – A rose-colored "Democratic Socialism" article said that, *"Socialism can be defined as 'a system of social organization in which private property and the distribution of income are subject to social control.*[33]*"* What is "social control" if we don't have it already? What doesn't our government control right now, today? Are socialists somehow saying that our government is not the social organization of everything from birth ID to death taxes?

See what happens when you don't pay your property tax. Or income and payroll tax, or any other tax. Try to build a house on your own property without a stack of permissions.

We can argue forever about the benefits of income redistribution and that mysterious ether called, "social justice." But if using "social control" of private property and distribution of income as the definition of socialism, then we've already got that, and democratic socialists should be satisfied.

But they're not satisfied, are they?

---

[32] People go to jail for fraud from every election cycle. Some cases, like LBJ's "Box 13 Scandal" have been audacious, well-known, and unpunished. But what do we do about it? (sound of crickets) *That* is really the issue.
[33] John Haltiwanger, Updated Feb 11, 2020, businessinsider.com/difference-between-socialist-and-democratic-socialist-2018-6

So, what do they *really* want?

Well, they want to be in charge whether others like it or not, as do most of us, sadly. That's how humans work. Most socialists want, in a broad and core-need sense, what the rest of us want.

- They may be angry and even violent toward their political foes; but most "socialists" say they want peace. World peace. As in …quit bombing people. That's a fine wish. Their rioters and saboteurs could try to exemplify that better, though.
- They want prosperity; however they define it. Their ideas on economics aside, who doesn't agree that people should prosper?
- They know our current social order is corrupt, and want corruption to go away. Who wouldn't agree with them on that? While the hard-left US House Rep. Alexandria Ocasio-Cortez has been accused of various corruptions herself, she's one of very few major party federal officeholders who's been outspoken against political corruption, and she's been rightly lauded for that.
- Socialists want their version of "fair." Yes, they do categorize people and promote special classes of rights and privileges based on these abstractions, and that is by any reasonable definition, anti-individualist and, yes, racist and sexist tribalism. But they still have a sense that things aren't fair now, and they're right about that.
- While they're unwittingly calling oppression down on all our heads, they think they're working toward freedom…personal freedom. That's a good goal, if by terrible means.

So, our problem with socialists isn't their goals; it's their chosen authoritarian plan to attain their goals. They're grabbing onto the same, ancient snake-oil political promises, and imagining that they're the newest Get Rich Quick scheme.

And to be fair, socialists often make very good arguments about western intervention in socialist nations like North Korea, Venezuela, Cuba and other descendants of the Russian revolutions of 1917. The arguments are at least based in fact. Our "progressive" Presidents T. Roosevelt and W. Wilson did tremendous damage to the world in making war into a grand adventure of Empire and corporate riches instead of self-defense only.

But the arguments that socialism quickly tears itself to bits are also rooted in fact. These arguments are strong enough that the peace, freedom and prosperity lovers among us should try to convince our fellows that what hasn't ever worked as advertised before…still won't work; and that the ideology responsible for the death of hundreds of millions, isn't as good as it sounds.

Socialist/ authoritarian ideology requires two things that non-socialists rightly detest:

1. Taking things away from people. Rights, property, options, opportunities. A few Central Planners determine everything for everybody. So people will want to fight back.
2. Violent force to stomp down those who fight back, or even talk back. We've seen way too much of that latter already. And aren't socialists the ones who first and most loudly (and often correctly) complain about police violence?

Certainly, the anti-authoritarians among us need to do better in presenting a better way to live than what any of us can see around us today. The "far right" Republican is no less authoritarian than the most "hard left" Democrat. They all want to clobber others, both foreign and domestic, into compliance with their tribal whims.

Does it matter whether we call Democrats Socialists and Republicans fascists when they both grow government power and eradicate our freedoms?

That brings us to a problem so serious that we won't fix any other problems until we address it…

There are Two Kinds of People

"The real division is not between conservatives and revolutionaries but between authoritarians and libertarians." – George Orwell, letter to Malcolm Muggeridge, 4 December 1948.

"There is nothing which I dread so much as a division of the republic into two great parties, each arranged under its leader, and concerting measures in opposition to each other." – John Adams, letter to Jonathan Jackson, 2 October 1780.

The "... kinds of people" shtick is good mostly for jokes – my favorite being: "There are 10 kinds of people – those who understand binary, and those who don't." Even in our seemingly binary political tribalism, the division is mostly a joke; a favorite being Tom Wolfe's, *"A liberal is a conservative who's been arrested. A conservative is a liberal who's been mugged."*

But it's true in only a very conditional sense that any of us are any one type of person, of course. Given the right circumstance, we can all be any type of saint or sinner. But there are, for the purposes of describing social dynamics relevant to this book, two conditional "types" between us; each with its pros and cons:

1. **Collectivists** – They prioritize the state (the "whole") over the individual. They exemplify both the positive and negative aspects of obedience to authority, which, most unfortunately, makes them the physical agents of tyranny. It's these people, who are both everyday

workers in peaceful civil society, and the arms and legs, judges, cops and soldiers of authoritarianism. They are the bureaucrats and administrators and enablers of oppression. They greatly outnumber the individualists. They are, as in Stanley Milgram's famous experiments on obedience to authority, "just doing my job" when the worst things in human history happen. But they can also be the self-sacrificing "team players," and even the pragmatic enablers of functional anarchy[34]. It's not bad to pursue the "good of the whole." But the theory and reality of that pursuit are starkly different. This book hopes a shift of perspective and new information can help nudge collectivists from the negative, to the positive aspects of their tendencies.

> **TALL POPPY SYNDROME** (tôl ˈpäpē ˈsinˌdrōm)
> A group-behavior phenomenon in which individuals who in any way stand apart from the flock or excel, are resented, criticized, feared, silenced and/ or ostracized. The working concept is that everyone should work both together and to common purpose — so those that stand out are cut down.

2. **Individualists** – In this context we're not talking about a mustached tough guy under a cowboy hat who's quick to buck trends, resist peer pressure, and care nothing of what others think. Here, individualists prioritize the individual over the state. Make no mistake about selfishness here; it's the individualists who are the Good Samaritans, personally doing what's right, *especially* when it's *against the rules.*

In a letter to Henry Lee, Thomas Jefferson articulated the two types from a different paradigm:

1. *"Those who fear and distrust the people, and wish to draw all powers from them into the hands of the higher classes."* – The "higher classes" here represent the state.

---

[34] This word has been too-often misapplied and conflated with "chaos." Anarchies, however limited in scope or scale, are groups that operate independently and free of centralized/ political force. – In short, self-governed societies, as in my first book, *"The Truth about Excelsior."*

2. *"Those who identify themselves with the people, have confidence in them, cherish and consider them as the most honest and safe..."* – In reality, Jefferson did not trust "the people" as much as he mistrusted the state.

Jefferson called his types, 1. "Aristocrat" (collectivists), and, 2. "Democrat" (individualists).

From an obviously more authoritarian perspective, Mao and many other outspoken Marxists claim the two types are the *proletariat* and the *bourgeoisie*. Or, "the people"/ "workers" (collectivists), versus the capitalists/ entrepreneurs (individualists). The problem is that in the Marxist world, there is no room for individualists.

That brings us back to Orwell's way to describe the two types as the two extremes on a political spectrum:

Libertarians (the political philosophy, not necessarily the party of the same name) are, by previous definition, individualist. Libertarianism prioritizes individuals over the state. The philosophy is often articulated as "fiscally conservative, socially liberal." But this is both oversimplified, and, given our continuous redefinition of "conservative" and "liberal," rather meaningless. A core principle of functional libertarianism is that no person *or group of persons* (i.e., government) has any right or authority to *initiate* aggression. Self-defense is of course a right – but initiating force against others, no matter who does it, is wrong. This is often called the NAP or Non-Aggression Principle. Libertarians, the ones who aren't anarchists anyway, believe that governments' only valid role is in the protection of individuals' rights, property, contracts and unowned, shared resources (e.g., air, water). If properly understood, most people would love a perfectly libertarian society. But it takes only a few of your authoritarian neighbors to prop up a king, and then everybody's got one, like it or not.

Authoritarians are, by definition, collectivist, since the "authority" is the abstraction of government taken to the extreme of all-powerful ruling entity. It seems inescapably insulting to call anybody an authoritarian. Most of us would claim we'd never serve a tyrant. But most humans did, do, and will pay taxes to, re-elect and obey authoritarian rulers. Consider how few people actually get off their derrière to in any way oppose tyrants. Perhaps you've seen the famous picture of brave, ill-fated August

Landmesser, the only man refusing to salute Hitler in a veritable sea of his obedient fellow countrymen. It was authoritarians/collectivists who drove the tanks at Tian'anmen Square, and pulled the triggers for Hitler, Stalin, Pol Pot and Mao. We tend to be pack animals, and obey Alphas. On the other hand, it has happened, and could happen again, that authoritarians live quite happily in a more libertarian society. However, under authoritarianism, the rights and property of individuals are by definition and force, taken for the "greater good." For example, labeling individuals and businesses "non-essential" and using armed force to make people comply with the lockdowns, mandates and prohibitions rationalized by COVID-19. The 17 Global Goals of the Great Reset are to be achieved by 2030 by means of global authoritarian rule, and elimination of individual rights. Not kidding. See globalgoals.org.

So… About our "Two-Party System…"

Is it representative of any two types of people previously described? Is it in fact representative of any two types of people we can imagine? By party rhetoric, one might be led to believe so. But that is bunk.

We've all heard of RINOs (Republicans In Name Only) and DINOs (Democrats In Name Only) and lately even LINOs (Libertarians In…well, you get the idea) that "don't belong" in their parties, according to people who probably do not belong in those parties themselves.

At a week-long county fair where we administered "The World's Smallest Political Quiz,"[35] the most "left-liberal," and "right-conservative" extremes were scored on the same day. The libertarian/ right test-taker was a Bible-believing, literal gun-toting (open-carry) Democrat. The progressive/ authoritarian was an officeholder with the local Republican Party. They certainly didn't fit their chosen parties' rhetoric and stereotype.

Our nation's founders had some things to say about such a scheme of mindlessly opposing tribes. Let's start with Mr. Jefferson. In a letter to

---

[35] A ten-question quiz created by Marshall Fritz, with scores placed on a graph originally devised by David Nolan, and now promoted by the Advocates for Self-Government at theadvocates.org/quiz/.

Francis Hopkinson, he wrote, "*I never submitted the whole system of my opinions to the creed of any party of men whatever... Such an addiction is the last degradation of a free and moral agent. If I could not go to heaven but with a party, I would not go there at all.*"

It's hard to find a founder more opposite Jefferson's views in general than Alexander Hamilton. But he wrote in Federalist #1, "*Nothing could be more ill-judged than that intolerant spirit which has, at all times, characterized political parties.*"

George Washington said in his 1796 Farewell Address: "*Let me now take a more comprehensive view and warn you in the most solemn manner against the baneful effects of the spirit of party, generally. This spirit, unfortunately, is inseparable from our nature, having its root in the strongest passions of the human mind. It exists under different shapes in all governments, more or less stifled, controlled, or repressed; but, in those of the popular form, it is seen in its greatest rankness and is truly their worst enemy. The alternate domination of one faction over another, sharpened by the spirit of revenge natural to party dissension, which in different ages and countries has perpetrated the most horrid enormities, is itself a frightful despotism. But this leads at length to a more formal and permanent despotism. The disorders and miseries which result gradually incline the minds of men to seek security and repose in the absolute power of an individual; and sooner or later the chief of some prevailing faction, more able or more fortunate than his competitors, turns this disposition to the purposes of his own elevation on the ruins of public liberty.*"

In other words, our founders, from federalist, antifederalist and even royalist persuasions, were opposed to political parties. Not just two political parties. *Any* political parties.

Yet the people of our new nation almost immediately spurned the warnings, and coagulated into, as feared, political factions.

Much of the problem is the same innate tribalism that infects every other aspect of humanity's politics. We tend to clump into arbitrary abstractions of club, clan, clique and face-painted, chest-bumping sports team. And as seen in today's parties of bitter contempt, there is genuine religious fervor in our "Two Party System."

And it was never just two. There have been many political sects throughout

USA history. For instance: Federalist, Democratic-Republican (not at all
the same as either D or R party today), National Republican, Democratic,
Whig, Republican, National Union...and these are just parties that once
elected a USA President.

There've been scores of other parties that won seats in the US Congress,
Gubernatorial and other offices; some with amusing names like Know
Nothing. Some with scary, odd or highly descriptive names like Anti-
Masonic, Readjuster or National Women's parties, were very successful in at
least some areas. There have been recent flash-in-the-pan parties like the
Reform Party that won a gubernatorial office among other offices, and then
all-but disappeared.

There have been many at least nominally unaffiliated, independent
candidates who've won offices up to US Senate …even today (i.e., Angus
King and Bernie Sanders).

Even within the two USA political parties that everybody knows about
today, there are wide differences in organization and even official name.
For example, the "Democratic Party" of Minnesota is actually the
Minnesota Democratic–Farmer–Labor Party (DFL), while the "Democratic
Party" of North Dakota is the North Dakota Democratic–Nonpartisan
League Party. And there are many sub-factions within the D and R parties
that are so opposed that they really oughtn't be party to their party at all –
today perhaps best-illustrated by Trumpist, Never-Trump, and the Texas
GOP versus Log Cabin Republicans.

So why do we think we have a Two-Party System in the USA?

We do not now, and never had a legal Two-Party System. It is in fact
unconstitutional by federal, and most state constitutions. We think we have
one because lots of people spread bunk from ignorance or corruption, and
far too many believe. There have been arguably six distinct party eras in the
USA, and only the last one offers any support to the existence of a "Two-
Party System:"

1. From 1792-1815, when Federalists and Anti-Federalists duked it out in
    comically nasty campaigns until the "Era of Good Feelings" under
    James Monroe and the new Democratic-Republican Party around 1815.

Yes, the words "Democratic" and "Republican" were once unified
under a single party banner. In this period, there weren't formally
organized political parties as we think of them today, but there were
opposing political factions. Hence all the dire warnings about political
parties from that era.

2. 1828-1854, when Whigs and the then-new Democratic Party
    predominated, and rising political power of those parties led to rising
    political corruption. There were still many other political parties, and
    many were regionally/locally successful.

3. 1854-1892, when slaving Democrats and the new, anti-slavery
    Republican Party, got truly bloody in our Civil War, with continued
    ugliness under Reconstruction and the seeds of Jim Crow. It was not
    so much a party era as it was an era of fundamental cultural transition,
    though it did see the organization and political success of the
    Republican Party. This was also when corporatism, or the creation of
    political entities called "corporations" were granted special powers and
    exemptions under law, including "human rights." The resulting power
    from the union of politics with these corporations, and the abuse of
    that power, prompted the rise of unions as a countering force, and the
    real beginning of "Special Interest Groups" for labor, big business,
    education and medicine.

4. "The Panic of 1893" through 1932 was a genuinely confused time
    when unparalleled economic and technological growth was churned
    with hubris, racism, corruption and socialism. Several Socialist parties
    (some still around today) were very successful, winning gubernatorial
    and mayoral races as well as seats in Congress and statehouses.
    Socialist Eugene Debs won 6% of the votes for President of the USA
    from his jail cell. Teddy Roosevelt embodied the tree-hugging, trust-
    busting, Big Government, global interventionist Progressives under the
    Bull Moose Party, and most Democrats (excepting some like Grover
    Cleveland) were the KKK and fat cat corporatists…hardly the image
    Democrats would associate themselves with today.

5. 1933-post WWII. The New Deal was a major turning point;
    particularly if any fidelity to the USA Constitution could be considered
    the Old Deal. And this was also one of the most significant turning
    points between the ideological identities of the Democratic and
    Republican parties. FDR, who admired and was admired by European

fascists and socialists, essentially stole the talking points and political power of the socialist, worker and labor parties. The Republican Party, as represented by "Mr. Republican" Senator Robert A Taft, opposed Teddy Roosevelt's authoritarianism, and was a much more libertarian and constitutional politician than would be popular in today's GOP. But WWII at least defeated the name, "socialism," and thus, by practical default, only the Democratic and Republican parties remained in positions of political power. The post-war years were critical to today, in that many previously powerful parties were flushed by the passions of war, leaving the Democratic and Republican parties in a powerful position to do what came next – that is to say, whatever they wanted.

6. 1964-today saw a whipsaw in Democrat versus Republican ideology so highly contentious and relatively recent that it's hard to trust historical sources which tend to have strong biases. But what's relevant to this chapter is that this was the era when Democrats and Republicans really joined hands and locked arms against voters with a fusillade of new rules and laws that restricted ballots and political party powers to only two parties. Fundamentally and critically, this era saw the rapid and nearly-universal rollout of Primary Elections in which only two parties can participate. The rest of this chapter will detail this a bit more. The short answer is that this was the actual beginning of a codified "Two-Party System" as we imagine it today. Please note, however that even aside from the illegalities and corruption detailed in following pages, independents and so-called "third parties" still win election to offices as high as Governor and US Senator, though the "laws" do keep getting more restrictive by the year.

Some insist that there is a logical, and voting-method reason for the predominance of only two parties called, "Duverger's Law." The French sociologist and politician, Maurice Duverger, deduced from his post-war observations that voting for only one candidate for offices for which there can be only one winner, tends to result in only two parties concentrating power. But as detailed above, the predominance of only two parties was quite recent to when he gathered his information. There was not necessarily any logical process at work, unless corruption can be considered a logical process. Duverger didn't even consider the laws already on the books that suppressed any competitors to the two that had the power to make laws.

Our Two-Party System is a corrupt mess, and most of us know that to at least some degree. We haven't reacted to it in any useful way because political power, and corruption that goes with it, has grown in stages, over several generations, in a sort of frog-in-the-cook-pot scenario. So discussing ideology or "issues" is a waste of time until we deal with this: The two private clubs called the Democratic and Republican Parties are:

- Corrupt organizations operating illegally, as substantiated in the following pages.
- Operated by pretty much the same few puppet masters. The small variation in owner pools (a few seemingly opposing corporations, unions, and "special interest groups") don't make any difference in political reality, because the major contributors/operators of both parties are the same bankers, military industrialists and energy, transportation, insurance, Big Ag, Big Pharma and increasingly as well as ominously, entertainment, information, education, technology and data powers, which are themselves controlled by a few immensely powerful globalists.

To banish any possibility of doubt about the preceding, what follows are examples from Indiana. Indiana has one of the better state constitutions, but is among the worst states in its anti-constitutional partisan, and separate but certainly not equal ballot access rules:

Indiana Constitution's Article I, Section 23 is very clear:

*"The General Assembly shall not grant to any citizen, **or class of citizens**, privileges or immunities, which, upon the same terms, shall not equally belong to all citizens."*

However, the far less concisely written Indiana Code[36]'s § 3-5-2-30 defines "Major political party" as "...*either of the two (2) parties whose nominees received the highest and second highest numbers of votes statewide for secretary of state in the last election.*" And then IC §§ 3-6-4.1-2 through 3-10-1-2, create arbitrary

---

36 The Brobdingnagian and ever-growing mass of rules only theoretically written under the "color of law."

thresholds that suppress all other candidates and political organizations, granting only Democratic and Republican party candidates taxpayer funded primary elections, which implicitly provide more money, public attention, free advertising and media promotion to only Democrats and Republicans, at the literal expense of all alternative parties and candidates.

Ind. Code § 6-4.1-4 specifies that members of the Indiana Election Commission "*must be a member of a major political party.*" And Ind. Code § 6-4.1-4 grants that only "*the state chairman of the major political party*" has powers of nomination and appointments for succeeding terms. Only designees "*of the state chairman of each of the major political parties*" shall "*serve as members of the state recount commission.*" (Ind. Code § 3-12-10-2.1) This is of course tremendous power unavailable to alternative parties and independent candidates.

Ind. Code § 3-10-1-4 grants only major political parties privileges of organization. Precinct committeeman, for example, are a special class of citizen who have special powers (e.g., Ind. Code § 3-13-1-4, 5, 6), yet aren't subject to the limitations placed on other political officeholders (Ind. Code § 3-6-1-15), and they're granted special powers and privileges for nomination to public office and filling vacancies (e.g., Ind. Code § 3-13-5, 6). Again, very powerful role unavailable to others who don't belong to the favored clubs.

Ind. Code § 3-10-1-15 sets apart a separate ticket for "*each political party holding a primary election*" making alternative candidates practically invisible to voters.

And to be clear…the Democratic and Republican Parties have, with the power they won after WWII, wrote themselves power over everybody else. Only *they* are "major political parties." Only *they* get all the taxpayer-funded promotion, special powers and exemptions. In other words, "…*privileges or immunities, which, upon the same terms, shall not equally belong to all citizens.*" In still other words, special deals for special people. Belonging to one of the two literally private clubs gives individuals special privileges, powers, immunities…and money, unavailable to anybody else.

Simply writing words into an ever-growing, multi-thousand-page State Code book does not make anything legitimate. Indiana Constitution's Article I, Section 25, for example, makes it clear that legislation cannot transgress the constitution:

"No law shall be passed, the taking effect of which shall be made to depend upon any authority, except as provided in this Constitution."

There's more in the federal constitution, detailed later, as well as other state constitutions and ongoing history, along with any sort of functional morality, to demonstrate that what we think is a Two-Party System is not at all how our society is supposed to work.

But do the two entrenched ruling clubs even represent who we are and what we believe?

The answer should be an easy "no." But in reality, our ideologies are apparently much more malleable than our tribal allegiances. Party loyalty is much more passion than logic. There's vast difference between what we say to pollsters versus how we vote. Approval rates for the US House of Representatives have averaged below 50% since the 1970's. From 2011 to 2015 the approval rates dipped into single digits. But US House reelection rates haven't dropped below 80% since the 1980's and have recently gone above 98%. And at all levels, local, state and federal, over 90% of us either actively or passively approve the status quo every Election Day. And that status quo is embodied in only two choices.

In what other area of life would we tolerate only two choices?

By whatever parameter one could imagine measuring this system, it's unconstitutional, immoral, destructive, divisive, generally disliked, and obviously not working. We really ought to stop sustaining it with our votes.

Do we really *want* a Two-Party System? We seem to hate it, but most voters vote for it every time.

You want a quick, simple fix to most of our society's problems? Here it is: Stop voting for this unconstitutional, corrupt, inherently divisive mess. Vote for alternatives and/or be an alternative yourself.

The crony network running the Two-Party System already has your money and everything else but your vote. Deny them that, and there'll be change.

It Takes a Village...*Not Government*

"It is not from the benevolence of the butcher, the brewer, or the baker that we expect our dinner, but from their regard to their own interest." — Adam Smith, *An Inquiry into the Nature and Causes of the Wealth of Nations,* bk. 1, ch. 2 (1776)

"Civil government, so far as it is instituted for the security of property, is in reality instituted for the defense of the rich against the poor, and for the defense of those who have property against those who have none." — Adam Smith, *An Inquiry into the Nature and Causes of the Wealth of Nations,* vol. 1, bk. 5, ch. 1 (1776)

"How can anyone read history and still trust politicians?" — Thomas Sowell, *Barbarians inside the Gates and Other Controversial Essays,* 1999

"*America is great because she is good, and if America ever ceases to be good, she will cease to be great"* is a saying typically attributed to that pro-American Frenchman, Alexis de Tocqueville. It's an interesting saying, but de Tocqueville probably never said it. Also, the saying itself is only partially true.

USA citizens have always been humans; not so different from all those sinners in France. A seed of truth in the quote is that there was a time when Americans[37] had to *act* hat-tipping, help-your-neighbor civil. There was a time when Americans, for the most part, *acted* better than they *were*.

During de Tocqueville's visit to the USA (1831), and in fact through the hundred-some years until Income Tax, central banking and the New Deal changed all the rules, churches were the Department of Health, Education and Welfare – even in our biggest cities. Churches ran hospitals, schools, welfare and social cooperative programs. It was church mothers who'd helped rear our young. It was church fathers and sons who'd helped at planting time. It was church leaders who'd opposed slavery and unscrupulous businesses, and it was the church that served as FEMA for natural disasters.

So excommunication meant the loss of key social services from the collective. If an uncivil, excommunicated person's barn burnt down, perhaps there'd be no enthusiastic church-based barn-raising to rebuild it.

The only alternatives to churches in those days were fraternal societies/clubs that *also* operated on a voluntary basis, and which *also* operated by moral code.

> In other words, to get social services and insurance from nothing more than a voluntary collection plate, Americans **had to behave**.

That was not such a bad thing! Per capita crime rates in cities, some of which were more densely populated a hundred years ago than now, were only a tiny fraction of what we have today even in rural areas. Murder was rare, big news when even kids walked around with firearms, and it was perfectly OK to fire your machine gun with a silencer before dressing up for church.

But now, instead of a voluntary tithe, Americans apparently prefer to give up more than half their wealth, time and purchasing power to a government that itself has neither interest nor experience in what most of us would call "morality." The combination of tax laws that gag preachers and policies

---

[37] Using "American" to describe USA-branded people. Canadians, Mexicans, Argentinians, etc., are Americans, too.

that replace traditional church roles have made churches socially irrelevant; and have made politicians our new gods.[38]

Fortunately for some, these politicians are for sale. Unfortunately for the rest of us, our politicians have been bought. Such corruption of power is as ancient as Cain and as unavoidable as death.

And that corrupt monster of involuntary force and involuntary association has also all-but-replaced any society's most fundamental cooperative organization…the family.

It's true that much of our nation's success was from broken treaties, stolen land and, at least a little, from slave labor[39]. But our nation became the envy of the world by constitutionally limiting the size and scope of political power, and allowing individuals (granted, not *all* individuals) to succeed. That was the Old Deal…politicians on a leash. And that old deal is *still* the *newest* deal in human history.

But since the "New Deal," we've devolved to more regulation, taxation and litigation than all other nations on earth …combined. And we must compete with nations that now have far less of all of that. …Even authoritarian nations like China.

There are no unions, EPA, OSHA, FDA, no patent enforcement or minimum wage in China, yet we buy things made there. Canada, the UK and Europe remove their VAT and GST taxes before shipping goods to our stores.

So, while we pat ourselves on the back for the USA's "progressive" benevolence, we're promoting slavery, unregulated pollution, disease, oppressive regimes and powerful enemies all over the world. When we buy

---

[38] This was not without church collaboration. The "Christian Socialist" movement of the late 1800's/early 1900's bears much of the blame for giving churches' social role unto Caesar.

[39] "The 1619 Project" authors have claimed that ~50% of the South's economy was from slave production, but it was actually ~5%. Still very significant, but it's important to understand that slave labor is ultimately very inefficient in the creation of general wealth.

shoes from Portugal, medical equipment from Germany or telecom service from France (*Sacré bleu!*), it's not at all that we're firing Americans (we're not; though that's another story). But we are, at least, rewarding those who don't bear the burden of USA taxation, regulation and litigation…and thereby punishing those of our own people who do suffer these burdens.

A better model is described by III John 1:11: "*Beloved, do not imitate evil but imitate good.*" Policy that rewards cooperation and discourages bad behavior doesn't make better people, really, but can make us act like better people. If that's the best we could do, great; because it's the best that's ever been done on any cultural scale.

But if we don't cut our politicians, their regulations, litigation and taxation down to competitive, and, by the way, *legal* size – and if we don't restore our better, more fundamental units of organization, from the individual, the family, and on up to the nation – we will not only cease to be great; we may just cease to be.

The FED: Potemkin Village on The Hill

"Paper money has had the effect in your state that it will ever have, to ruin commerce, oppress the honest, and open the door to every species of fraud and injustice." — George Washington to J. Bowen, 1787.

"Regarding the Great Depression. You're right, we did it. We're very sorry. But thanks to you, we won't do it again." — Ben Bernanke, 2002 speech conceding that Milton Friedman and Anna Schwartz were correct in their 1963 analysis blaming the Fed for the Great Depression.

"When He had made a whip of cords, He drove them all out of the temple, with the sheep and the oxen, and poured out the changers' money and overturned the tables." — John 2:15, New King James version

It's a common pastime of libertarian wonks to argue which of our governments' many lies is the biggest, most fraudulent, and/or most destructive. War seems obvious to most people, as truth is always the first casualty, and deaths come by the millions. Perhaps, in fact, humanity's first Big Lie is that we need our kings to protect us from other people's kings (I Samuel 8:6-20). But war is only a symptom of already existing antisocial disease (a symptom of that fruit Adam and Eve ate in Eden?), and waging war has major prerequisites: money, and the ability to raise it with *debt*, being the key. So looking at this in a fundamental, moral and foundational fashion, it's hard to imagine any single corruption of modern times that has had a more profoundly destructive effect than The Fed's literal monopoly money, as the enabling, sustaining engine of almost all other of today's corruptions…including transgenerational theft, and never-ending war.

On one hand it may seem too much to evoke Christ's act of Holy violence against the moneychangers defiling the Temple. But with the transgenerational and global deception, theft, and enablement of vast corruption, war, debt and malinvestment initiated by the debasement of our monetary system, our Federal Reserve System, as it exists today, must be among Lucifer's most clever work.

> Short answer: Today, The Fed literally makes "money" from nothing more than debt, charging multiply-compounded interest at a literal rate of infinity, for the benefit of politicians and banks, and at ever-greater cost…to the rest of us. Our government demands its use under extreme threats not only in the USA, but globally as well, making it, by definition, monopoly money. It's the worst of both Big Business greed, and Big Government corruption, and it is eating away at our standard of living, our culture, and will almost surely destroy this nation if we can't kill it.

I'd already devoted a chapter to some monetary history and effect in my previous book, "The Truth about Excelsior,"[40] that I'll not repeat here. And there are of course innumerable books on the subjects of monetary theory, monetary/fiscal policy and banking. I highly (highly) recommend G. Edward Griffin's *"Creature from Jekyll Island."*

But just a bit of explanation is necessary if we're to find a common-ground understanding of today's inflation, as well as many other fundamental problems of ungoverned government.

By our federal constitution, only the U.S. Congress is authorized in Article I, Section 8:5, *"To coin Money, regulate the Value thereof, and of foreign Coin, and*

---

[40] A fantasy story intended to be fun yet still thought-provoking with both fact and reasonable conjecture.

fix the Standard of Weights and Measures." The constitution's authors were very insistent upon coined money, or specie, because they'd already experienced disasters with paper money, debt instruments and bank notes. The reason for tying the value of money to elected representatives was that voters could thus punish fiscal/monetary irresponsibility every Election Day. Congress, via the Treasury, still coins money (though coins are no longer made from metal of corresponding market value). But the value of both coins, paper and digital tender, as well as the fundamental policies by which *all* money works within this country, has been unconstitutionally delegated away without constitutionally provided oversight.

Since 1913, USA currency and our federal monetary policy has been created and governed by a quasi-private, para-political cabal called the Federal Reserve Bank (FRB) or Federal Reserve System, though typically called "The Fed."

The original Federal Reserve Act, while produced by an unconstitutional and thieving cartel, was a remarkably clever bit of sophistry for a collusion between nefarious banksters and corrupt and/or clueless politicians. Its complexity made it seem like it must be too sophisticated for us simple folk to comprehend:

- 12 regional "private" stock-issuing banks, each governed by "local" bankers (with foreign influence and ownership…but that's another story).
- A central Board of Governors comprised of seven term-limited officers (14 years) appointed by the POTUS and confirmed by the US Senate.
- Each bank required to keep 6% of its capital in its regional reserve bank, for which it gets a corresponding number of fixed-price, non-resalable shares of the FRB stock, along with Fed system voting rights, and a fixed 6% yearly dividend.
- The Fed, being astoundingly profitable, isn't supposed to keep the profits in excess of what's paid to member banks' dividends. Instead, that money goes to the US Treasury.
- None of today's "dual mission" rhetoric and purported role in determining inflation and interest rates was any part of this. The original design and *stated* mission were to be a "lender of last resort"

for crashes and banking emergencies, and to (and this is how it was sold to politicians) provide our central government with a constant flow of money. In reality, of course, the core mission was to privatize bank profits, socialize risk, and keep politicians happy with the scam. In other words – make taxpayers bail out the biggest banks when their riskiest bets go bust, and give politicians enough money for… whatever floats their boats of war and corruption.

- Many claim that Fractional Reserve Banking, or keeping only a percentage of assets as cash on premises, is the core evil. It is evil if it's based on fraud; but it's the fraud itself that's the core evil. Of course banks should to hold sufficient assets as cash on hand as a reserve for bank runs and so on. But banks make a lot of money by loaning out the stuff. So there is incentive for banks to invest in debt, or loan out more money than has been deposited, as cash in a vault doesn't earn them any dividends or interest. So the Fed's reserve requirement of minimum reserves on member banks was a *good thing*. But, remember, the "money" they lend is created from nothing. They hand you something with no intrinsic value, charge interest on it, and take your real stuff if you don't pay them back. So fractional reserve banking with fake money actually is evil. And during COVID, the reserve requirements were dropped to…zero.

- If you look up the "Cantillon Effect," whereby people closer to the creation of the money get rich at the expense of everybody else, you'll see how the Fed is great for making "investment-class" people richer, while, unfortunately, making the rest of us poorer. It was already the case that the Fed's "fiat currency," or paper money made "legal" by banking and "legal tender" laws made by politicians (though still unconstitutional), was a hidden tax. Every dollar printed made every dollar in circulation worth less and less.

- But we ordinary folk were still free to trade and even pay taxes with real money, as there were still actually-constitutional gold, silver, nickel and copper coins in circulation. So, for a while, business was good, life was good. Being a USA citizen was…pretty great!

All of that quickly got worse after The Fed's big monetary mistake, or printing too much money during a period of lower economic output (Friedman called it, "too much money chasing too few goods"), which caused the 1929 crash. Since there are many books on that subject, and there's no good reason to detail it here, what follows are relevant facts about the changes that followed:

1. April 5, 1933, FDR demanded, by unconstitutional Executive Order, that all gold coins, and gold certificates in denominations of more than $100, be turned in for paper currency only nominally backed by the purloined gold. In other words, in violation of the federal, and many states' constitutions' prescription for sound money based on inherently limited and therefore precious gold and/or silver, FDR suspended most trade of specie, or metal of some inherent value, in favor of paper fiat currency – or money of only politically decreed, or "fiat" value.

2. Freed from the constraint of gold's inherently limited supply, the Banking Act of 1935 rewrote the rules, reorganized and centralized the structure, changed the titles and expanded the powers and functions of The Fed. This transformed The Fed into an engine of nearly endless political IOUs, and of course, profits from debt. It was, thereafter, a system that monetizes and markets debt by printing paper money of only politically-promised "fiat currency."

3. The central banking crisis and global Great Depression was hard on every nation's money. After shoring up the British Pound with a temporary gold standard, Churchill dropped the standard in 1931, and the pound dropped ~30% to the US dollar. During WWII, knowing that the pound was entirely unbacked, Germany's "Operation Bernhard" nearly broke England's economy with a scheme of forging British pound notes. After all, too much of anything always reduces the value of each. And when the value of each is already a tenuous act of public faith, such damage will always be severe. That should've been a lesson to the world, including us. But it wasn't.

4. Initially, and for a while, the paper money issued by The Fed was partly "backed" by actual deposits of monetary metal specie (i.e., gold and silver). The USA, largely through the Lend/Lease program and weapons sales, had in fact acquired around ¾ of the world's monetary gold supply prior to our entry into WWII. Bankers sold credit and Ford sold engines to even Hitler. War is very profitable when only supplying other nations' wars. So the USA acquired much of the globes' monetary gold supply very quickly. This, along with #3 above, and the economic boost from manufacturing activity as a supplier of global warfare (see War is a Racket, by General Smedley Butler), made the US dollar (USD) something of the new Reserve

Currency, or global money standard, by the default of the British Pound.

5. The Bretton Woods Agreement of 1944 attempted to stabilize world currencies to the USD by at least nominally pegging the dollar to a conditional "gold standard" by which the 44 allied, signatory nations could exchange dollars for gold at fixed exchange rates. This seemed good for the USA, but ultimately doomed us by a phenomenon called the "Triffin Paradox" (which you can look up online). Short answer: our dollar hegemony doomed us to increasing inflation and desperate means to maintain the dollar, and, ultimately decreasing standard of living for most USA citizens before the whole thing falls apart …which will happen fairly soon, unfortunately.

6. In 1967, Charles de Gaulle called the bluff on the USA's gold reserves. He claimed we'd spent it all on our wars and new social programs, and were just printing monopoly paper in what the French Minister of Finance Valéry Giscard d'Estaing famously called "*exorbitant privilege.*" Because de Gaulle was right, US President Johnson officially ended the "gold cover" or 25% gold reserve backing in 1968. This prompted something of a global run on the bank. So, US President Nixon unilaterally cancelled the "asymmetric financial system" charade by unilaterally suspending the Breton Woods Agreement in 1971 on the claim that the suspension would be only temporary. It wasn't.

7. In the midst of the inevitable high inflation that followed, along with an oil crisis caused by problems in the Middle East largely created by us, the Nixon administration thought it very clever to arrange with OPEC and the House of Saud what's now called the "petrodollar system," by which OPEC oil must be purchased with USD. This created both a market for USD, and a bedfellow alliance with terrorists and strong links to most of today's real enemies.

8. The problems with the preceding, along with the costs of "Great Society" and following programs, and the ballooning War On Drugs, led to the Federal Reserve Reform Act of 1977, which completely changed the intended function of the bank. From this "reform," the stated function became, 1. "Price stability," or inflation targets by, theoretically, the creation and destruction of fiat currency, and 2. Managing interest rates, in order to monetize the rapidly growing

political power, programs and debt of a government that was exploding in size and global tentacles. Ironically, both interest rates and inflation hit all-time highs by 1980. And, while this isn't the place to explain it, the Fed became debt engine of not only the USA, but also the whole world, via global banking systems. (see the aforementioned book, "The Creature from Jekyll Island")

9. FDIC-insured institutions (that taxpayers would bail out- really. That's how it was always intended to work) had previously been required to hold 10% above their low reserve tranche on hand as a reserve fraction to avoid bank run crashes. The Fed dropped this previously required reserve fraction to zero in 2020 in response to COVID-19 politics.

10. Also, in response to virus-rationalized mandates, prohibitions, lockdowns and massive purchases of virus-related injections and treatment subsidies, our government ran up debt and The Fed ran the money presses bigly, spiking both debt and devaluation of currency that led to today's inflation spike; by far the highest since 1980. Nobel Prize-winning economist Milton Friedman said that, *"Inflation is always and everywhere a monetary phenomenon, in the sense that it is and can be produced only by a more rapid increase in the quantity of money than in output."* The Fed actually *increased* the supply of money when there was *decreased* economic output. …Like what happened right before the Great Depression.

11. The national debt is of course higher than ever if accurately reported by any measure – public or private held, by GDP, and certainly when including unfunded mandates that didn't even exist in the previous post-WWII high.

The *theory* of central banking, like the theory of centralized power of any kind, is, theoretically, rational, if it's not primarily a cartel to swindle taxpayers, that is. Theoretically, a central bank that issues stable, sound currency, keeps its quantity limited and correlated to economic output, and even one that funds governments directly, should work. Even what we call "real money," like gold and silver, no matter how naturally limited, historically stable, and even useful as industrial metal, carries only the value agreed upon by users of the money and metal. "Money[41]" is an instrument of value exchange…and trust. If everybody agrees to use it for the exchange of goods and services, and if they trust that the medium is in some way authentic and correlates to some measure of value, then it doesn't matter whether money is a scrap of paper backed by nothing, a seashell, a gold coin, an animal or even a carved stick. All the preceding things have been used in trade.

If everybody, everywhere on the planet, used a single, agreed-upon unit of money or currency like easily verifiable weights of gold, then global currency wars and domestic currency manipulation as we have today, would be impossible. Billionaires like conservatives' favorite antichrist, George Soros, as well as sex trafficker Jeffrey Epstein (associated with everybody, including Donald Trump – who admires Soros!), made billions trading currencies, while the rest of us paid for it through inflation and transferred wealth, because all nations have their own currency schemes. We've a whole political/economic dynasty build on the gaming of money.

But when the money or currency, whatever its form, is manipulated for the wrong reasons and to an unsustainable degree, severe oppression (like serfdom or slavery) and violence (like wars hot and cold, coups and "color revolutions") will result.

The Fed operates free, or they like to say *"independent,"* of regulation or external audits as would apply to other corporations (except vaccine manufacturers…but that's a whole other Pandora's Box). And these central moneychangers and their cronies don't have to answer questions if they don't want to. Which may seem fine, because their answers are often self-contradictory gobbledygook. On purpose.

But this is not fine. The Fed has become, more than anything else, and fundamentally, an enabler of transgenerational debt for the masses, and transfer of wealth to the few.

It is exceptionally dangerous to mix capitalist profit motivation with political force and politically-granted monopoly. Such hybrids end up

---

[41] Ignoring the varying definitions of money, currency, specie, etc.

amplifying the worst of both businesses released from accountability to the market, and politicians freed of accountability by delegation to unaccountable and unseen financier/plutocrats. When a few people are granted a monopoly in determining what money is and who can make it, and when their system generates money from debt, as is the case with today's Fed… there will be, and is today, trouble.

Wars are of course the biggest single debt and money makers, since, as James Madison pointed out: *"War is the parent of armies; from these proceed debts and taxes; and armies and debts and taxes are the known instruments for bringing the many under the domination of the few. No nation can preserve its freedom in the midst of continual warfare. …In war, the public treasuries are to be unlocked; and it is the executive hand which is to dispense them."*

And it's grimly ironic that now, with all the litigating, ballyboohooing and campaigning against "big business," "special interest" groups and "monopolistic business practices," the most dangerous industry of all, the biggest of them all – central/political monopoly banking, is completely unregulated, monitored or even generally recognized as a root threat.

In a letter to John Taylor in 1816, T. Jefferson wrote, *"And I sincerely believe with you, that banking establishments are more dangerous than standing armies; & that the principle of spending money to be paid by posterity, under the name of funding, is but swindling futurity on a large scale."*

But the lessons of history die with those who lived it.

As it's obvious that even with a good initial design, relatively speaking, the power and potential for corruption was too great. It was always unconstitutional, and it's now enormously destructive.

It's time to End the Fed.

But, of course, the only way to do that is to elect politicians who agree.

So, where're we now?

"A general Dissolution of Principles & Manners will more surely overthrow the Liberties of America than the whole Force of the Common Enemy. While the People are virtuous they cannot be subdued; but when once they lose their Virtue they will be ready to surrender their Liberties to the first external or internal Invader." — Samuel Adams, letter to James Warren, February 12, 1779.

"Whom the gods would destroy they first make mad." — Ancient sentiment, multiple attributions.

Our species had previously only dreamed of comforts such as we enjoy today. Our engineers, inventors, entrepreneurs and people of every other description from bartenders to roofers, from musicians to massage therapists, have given us wonderful means of extending lives, educating and entertaining minds, creating dizzying options in exotic spices, comfortable clothes and housing, while increasing productivity, lowering costs, and even promoting relative peace. In the USA, most of the poorest among us are more comfortable than kings of times past. And despite recently rising crime rates, that mayhem is still not as bad as during the early 1970's to early 1990's. Despite our nation's many and damning flaws, we're still among the world's most fair and globally benevolent nations, ever. Our standard of living is almost embarrassingly high, even in comparison to European standards.

We have good reason to believe we've got it good. It's understandable that our cultural attitude seems to be, "don't rock the boat."

But in exactly that way, these are not unprecedented times. While our art, music, science and technology have, at least since the fall of Rome, been mostly upwardly progressive, humanity's political organizations are tediously predictable, with an eventual 100% failure rate – often catastrophic – as demonstrated throughout our history, everywhere on the planet. And there are no indications that, as a species, collectively, we've learned anything from this.

There have been plenty of Cassandras[42] warning us of impending doom all along, of course. Many have for millennia correctly foretold our species' inevitable wars, crashes, monetary and fiscal follies, political upheavals and cultural crises. The people who turn out to be correct outnumber the mighty few who're leading our societies, and who are almost always, and often hilariously, wrong.[43]

And yet…

What is this doom of which they speak? Is it really doom, or just the cyclic waves of too-rare good behavior and the more mundane bad behavior from our problematic species? Didn't kids still play and laugh during the Dark Ages, the Great Depression, and the World Wars? Didn't some people still prosper, make love, and build a good life in the worst of times? And don't we all die ultimately anyway? Has there ever really been a true Golden Age? At every time in human history there's been a favored class and an underclass. And while we may change terminology and specifics, we've always had rulers, and the ruled.

And, just as today, political leaders have always tried to simultaneously

---

[42] Trojan priestess both empowered and cursed by Apollo to accurately prophesy the future, but not be believed.

[43] Like Nobel Prize-winning economist Paul Krugman's prediction that the internet would be no more impactful than the fax machine. Or longtime incumbent Congressman Hank Johnson's concerns that Guam would "…*tip over and capsize.*" Examples abound.

scare us, and yet tell us they've got it all under control. That's how they both rationalize and obtain power over us.

> **Gaslighting** - gas·light·ing | \ ˈgas-ˌlī-tiŋ - Psychological manipulation over time that causes victims to question their own thoughts, memory, senses and perception of reality, leading to dependency on the perpetrator. — From the1938 stage play *Gas Light*, and two later movies called *Gaslight*.

It's a sad comedy that in today's politics, there is no advantage to being right, and no demerit in being wrong. Political promises, and delivered reality, are totally disconnected, with no public expectation of anything better. Our ever-reliable votes of continuous reelection empower and justify the wrong, rewarding them with power, notoriety, money, and plenty of promotion in all the popular "He said/ She said[44]" media.

Visionary economist Thomas Sowell said, *"It is hard to imagine a more stupid or more dangerous way of making decisions than by putting those decisions in the hands of people who pay no price for being wrong."*

Unfortunately, such few prominent people like Sowell who have been, and are still now almost always correct, are in that sorry tribe that mainstream media wonks and professional politicos of both major political tribes call, "fringe," "wackos," "losers," or when more erudite in their insults, "heterodox.[45]" Perhaps a part of the problem is that it's easy to spew foolishness, hard to resist believing it; yet it's an obviously elusive talent to be able to warn people of danger in actionable time without sounding like Chicken Little or an irascible curmudgeon.

Nevertheless, We The People need warning. But then, what is human history but a never-ending litany of warnings?

It was over 230 years ago that innumerable American politicians, wonks

---

[44] Today's sad state of "fact-checking" and partisan journalism is a whole other book.

[45] Often applied to "Austrian School" economists who are often proven correct, yet are political outcasts.

and economists warned us of the dangers of paper money, Central Banks and their inherently dangerous and corrupting monetary alchemy…as well as the danger of standing armies and perpetual war. It has been nearly as long since George Washington warned us of the danger of political parties and their battling factions. It's about a hundred years ago that Fiorello LaGuardia warned us about the need to police the police during the first Prohibition against booze. General/ President Eisenhower warned us around 60 years ago about not only the military industrial complex, but also the danger "…*that public policy could itself become the captive of a scientific-technological elite.*" Since practically its beginning, the CIA was working hand-in-glove with mob bosses. Over 50 years ago we found that our CIA was funding student radicals; and over 40 years ago, the CIA was caught paying our news media to lie…about the CIA's own murderous shenanigans, among other things. In more recent years we learned, many times, that our government lies about spying on everybody, and about the justification and backward progress of our endless wars. If the recent years' gaslighting and paid-for lies taught us anything, it's that lies and subversion are Standard Operating Procedure at every level, and on both embarrassingly partisan sides, of our bureaucratic state.

So today, militant groups such as Proud Boys and AntiFa have risen up as proxy armies for the anti-constitutional two-headed monster of tribal fear and loathing we call the "Two-Party System."

Their spasms of partisan spite have created amazing cognitive dissonance.

Democrats want massive government, but not the police who enforce it. Republicans want guns to fight oppressive government, but idolize the militarized police they'd have to fight. Probably all of us have seen the two opposing yard signs – "Had Enough? Vote Democratic!" "Had Enough? Vote Republican!"

Even a quick glance at the rate of government expansion in debt, spending, pages added to the federal code books, or any consideration of foreign entanglements, abuse, and corruption of power, shows that Democratic and Republican Party administrations are indistinguishable.

Fool me once, shame on you; fool me twice, shame on me. We the People have fooled ourselves every Election Day. We have said too many things with our mouths that we've upended with our votes.

Unfortunately, there is a tragic misunderstanding about the purpose of elections and the power of our votes. Elections are not for hiring politicians. For millennia and everywhere, there are still politicians where there are no elections. Our founders bequeathed us, at great cost, the ability to freely and safely choose our own government.

But they meant elections as a flush lever, not as a hiring process, and certainly not as a poker chip in a game of odds. As already mentioned previously, our elections are the power of *peaceful* revolution, so that we don't have to have that *other* kind…

So where are we now? The warning signs are everywhere. Our culture and previously cherished freedom are all but gone. The silk glove has already come off the iron fist of state.

What is it that gentlemen wish? What would they have? Is life so dear, or peace so sweet, as to be purchased at the price of chains and slavery? Forbid it, Almighty God! I know not what course others may take; but as for me, give me liberty or …

How about we try constitutional rule of law?

Annotated Declaration of Independence

"Violence is not necessary to destroy a civilization. Each civilization dies from indifference toward the unique values which created it." — Nicolás Gómez Dávila, *Escolios a un texto implicito: Obra completa,* 2006

"Here was buried Thomas Jefferson, author of the Declaration of American Independence, of the Statute of Virginia for Religious Freedom, and Father of the University of Virginia."
— Thomas Jefferson's epitaph, written by Thomas Jefferson, omitting that he was also the President of the United States of America

> My annotations are in a box like this one.   Everything else following is the text of the Declaration of Independence, as written.
>
> This Declaration was similar in structure, tradition and purpose to at least two previous petitions made by British subjects: the Petition of Right, and the Grand Remonstrance.

The unanimous Declaration of the thirteen united States of America

When in the Course of human events, it becomes necessary for one people to dissolve the political bands which have connected them with another, and to assume among the powers of the earth, the separate and

equal station to which the Laws of Nature and of Nature's God entitle
them, a decent respect to the opinions of mankind requires that they
should declare the causes which impel them to the separation.

We hold these truths to be self-evident, that all men are created equal, that
they are endowed by their Creator with certain unalienable Rights, that
among these are Life, Liberty and the pursuit of Happiness.--That to
secure these rights, Governments are instituted among Men, deriving their
just powers from the consent of the governed, --That whenever any Form
of Government becomes destructive of these ends, it is the Right of the
People to alter or to abolish it, and to institute new Government, laying its
foundation on such principles and organizing its powers in such form, as
to them shall seem most likely to effect their Safety and Happiness.

Prudence, indeed, will dictate that Governments long established should
not be changed for light and transient causes; and accordingly all
experience hath shewn, that mankind are more disposed to suffer, while
evils are sufferable, than to right themselves by abolishing the forms to
which they are accustomed.

But when a long train of abuses and usurpations, pursuing invariably the
same Object evinces a design to reduce them under absolute Despotism,

it is their right, it is their duty, to throw off such Government, and to provide new Guards for their future security.--Such has been the patient sufferance of these Colonies; and such is now the necessity which constrains them to alter their former Systems of Government. The history of the present King of Great Britain is a history of repeated injuries and usurpations, all having in direct object the establishment of an absolute Tyranny over these States. To prove this, let Facts be submitted to a candid world.

> Replace "**_present King of Great Britain_**" with your least-favorite politician, and cogitate. Consider attention to what our founders called tyranny and cause for this declaration. It wasn't all as bad or extreme as many of us think. The average colonist was rich and privileged compared to most people around the world, including the "commoners" of England. Yet it is our **_duty_** to throw off a counterproductive, destructive government. Pay close attention to the itemized complaints that follow:

He has refused his Assent to Laws, the most wholesome and necessary for the public good.

> Our "federal" government routinely overturns state and local laws in violation of its charter. What's described in this book is just an illustrative sample of our politicians' transgressions of written law.

He has forbidden his Governors to pass Laws of immediate and pressing importance, unless suspended in their operation till his Assent should be obtained; and when so suspended, he has utterly neglected to attend to them.

> Consider how our central government, in violation of both state and federal constitutions, variously forbids, overrules and mandates rules and limitations against states. Food, drugs, education, infrastructure, private disaster relief, immigration and healthcare are just a few examples.

He has refused to pass other Laws for the accommodation of large districts of people, unless those people would relinquish the right of Representation in the Legislature, a right inestimable to them and formidable to tyrants only.

He has called together legislative bodies at places unusual, uncomfortable, and distant from the depository of their public Records, for the sole purpose of fatiguing them into compliance with his measures.

He has dissolved Representative Houses repeatedly, for opposing with manly firmness his invasions on the rights of the people.

He has refused for a long time, after such dissolutions, to cause others to be elected; whereby the Legislative powers, incapable of Annihilation, have returned to the People at large for their exercise; the State remaining in the mean time exposed to all the dangers of invasion from without, and convulsions within.

He has endeavoured to prevent the population of these States; for that purpose obstructing the Laws for Naturalization of Foreigners; refusing to pass others to encourage their migrations hither, and raising the conditions of new Appropriations of Lands.

He has obstructed the Administration of Justice, by refusing his Assent to Laws for establishing Judiciary powers.

He has made Judges dependent on his Will alone, for the tenure of their offices, and the amount and payment of their salaries.

He has erected a multitude of New Offices, and sent hither swarms of Officers to harrass our people, and eat out their substance.

He has kept among us, in times of peace, Standing Armies without the Consent of our legislatures.

He has affected to render the Military independent of and superior to the Civil power.

be. This Rubicon has been crossed, despite Eisenhower's warning against the "military-industrial complex." But in that same Farewell Address, Eisenhower warned of an "…*equal and opposite danger that public policy could itself become the captive of a* **scientific-technological elite**." That'd now include everything from the CIA/NSA to Facebook and Google that are now an even greater threat.

He has combined with others to subject us to a jurisdiction foreign to our constitution, and unacknowledged by our laws; giving his Assent to their Acts of pretended Legislation:

Think UN, NAFTA, various treaties transcending constitutional authority, executive agencies, etc., that delegate authority and powers never granted. But there's a lot more to discuss with this that won't fit here. Keep in mind that this was well-before the USA Constitution, or even the Articles of Confederation. The word "constitution" here is more moral/cultural than literal in the sense of a written, signed constitution.

For Quartering large bodies of armed troops among us;

We have for some time had much more force hidden from view in both internally-focused spies and armed force, than our government would advertise…until recently. Our black-clad storm troopers and their armored vehicles and military weapons can appear from seemingly nowhere, as seen during, for just one example, the aftermath of the Boston Marathon Bombing.

For protecting them, by a mock Trial, from punishment for any Murders which they should commit on the Inhabitants of these States;

Think of today's state of "internal investigations" by police and federal agencies like the FBI and IRS. Or even gruesome episodes like the burning deaths of adults and children at Waco. They typically find themselves innocent.

For cutting off our Trade with all parts of the world;

We're not being cut off in this sense. There are, on the other hand, innumerable unconstitutional regulations, crony treaties, restrictions, prohibitions and unfair subsidies / immunities made by corrupt (but

continuously reelected) incumbents and cronies, that put domestic
markets and companies at a competitive disadvantage, though.

For imposing Taxes on us without our Consent;

We have no excuses for today's dismal, complicated, corrupt condition of
our incomprehensible Tax Codes. Our reelection votes really do serve as
our consent.

For depriving us in many cases, of the benefits of Trial by Jury;

This has happened to the author and too many others who are even
denied "standing" in courts of law. But we have bigger problems with
our judicial system than even this.

For transporting us beyond Seas to be tried for pretended offences;

The whole point of the Guantanamo Bay detention camp is to transport
people outside our legal system for "special treatment."

For abolishing the free System of English Laws in a neighbouring
Province, establishing therein an Arbitrary government, and enlarging its
Boundaries so as to render it at once an example and fit instrument for
introducing the same absolute rule into these Colonies;

This is about the Quebec Act of 1774, which assimilated the previously
French colonies, and encouraged English citizens to populate and expand
Canada toward the other American colonies and into what's now our
Midwest. That Act prompted the Invasion of Quebec in 1775, by which
the colonists attempted to bring the Canadians to the colonists' side
against England. This was a very contentious set of conflicts, but there
probably isn't a clear analogue today.

For taking away our Charters, abolishing our most valuable Laws, and
altering fundamentally the Forms of our Governments;

Where do we start on the perversion, inversion and destruction of
constitutional rule of law? That's what this book's all about.

For suspending our own Legislatures, and declaring themselves invested with power to legislate for us in all cases whatsoever.

He has abdicated Government here, by declaring us out of his Protection and waging War against us.

He has plundered our seas, ravaged our Coasts, burnt our towns, and destroyed the lives of our people.

He has constrained our fellow Citizens taken Captive on the high Seas to bear Arms against their Country, to become the executioners of their friends and Brethren, or to fall themselves by their Hands.

He has excited domestic insurrections amongst us, and has endeavoured
to bring on the inhabitants of our frontiers, the merciless Indian Savages,
whose known rule of warfare, is an undistinguished destruction of all ages,
sexes and conditions.

In every stage of these Oppressions We have Petitioned for Redress in the
most humble terms: Our repeated Petitions have been answered only by
repeated injury. A Prince whose character is thus marked by every act
which may define a Tyrant, is unfit to be the ruler of a free people.

Nor have We been wanting in attentions to our Brittish brethren. We
have warned them from time to time of attempts by their legislature to
extend an unwarrantable jurisdiction over us. We have reminded them of
the circumstances of our emigration and settlement here. We have
appealed to their native justice and magnanimity, and we have conjured
them by the ties of our common kindred to disavow these usurpations,
which, would inevitably interrupt our connections and correspondence.
They too have been deaf to the voice of justice and of consanguinity. We
must, therefore, acquiesce in the necessity, which denounces our
Separation, and hold them, as we hold the rest of mankind, Enemies in
War, in Peace Friends.

We, therefore, the Representatives of the united States of America, in
General Congress, Assembled, appealing to the Supreme Judge of the
world for the rectitude of our intentions, do, in the Name, and by
Authority of the good People of these Colonies, solemnly publish and
declare, That these United Colonies are, and of Right ought to be Free
and Independent States; that they are Absolved from all Allegiance to the
British Crown, and that all political connection between them and the
State of Great Britain, is and ought to be totally dissolved; and that as
Free and Independent States, they have full Power to levy War, conclude
Peace, contract Alliances, establish Commerce, and to do all other Acts
and Things which Independent States may of right do. And for the
support of this Declaration, with a firm reliance on the protection of
divine Providence, we mutually pledge to each other our Lives, our

Fortunes and our sacred Honor.

Our nation's foundational documents, particularly those written by the so-called "anti-federalists," present an entirely different picture of state and individual sovereignty than we're taught in government schools or gather from today's media.

What follows are the laws intended to restrain our government, and thus guarantee our liberties. While it's important to know our rights, it's even more important to know the legal restraints on those who could take our rights away.

And let's not fool ourselves. Words of law, like words of love and war, require action for their effect. So, yes, the constitutions, state and federal, are supposed to be stout leashes on around the neck of our politicians. But it is We The People who must hold the other end of that leash.

Annotated USA Constitution

"...a wise and frugal Government, which shall restrain men from injuring one another, shall leave them otherwise free to regulate their own pursuits of industry and improvement, and shall not take from the mouth of labor the bread it has earned. This is the sum of good government, and this is necessary to close the circle of our felicities." — Thomas Jefferson's First Inaugural Address, 4 March 1801

"If men were angels, no government would be necessary." — James Madison or maybe Alexander Hamilton, Federalist No. 51, the *New York Packet*, February 8, 1788

*"But when they said, **"Give us a king to lead us,"** this displeased Samuel; so he prayed to the LORD. And the LORD told him: "Listen to all that the people are saying to you; it is not you they have rejected, but they have rejected me as their king."* — Old Testament, I Samuel 8: 6-7

"The secular corollary to 'In God We Trust' is that, 'In Politicians, We Do Not." — Andrew Horning, 1996

Introduction to the annotated Constitution

Following this introduction is the complete, current United States Constitution, with the author's annotations that many have found useful as shared online and in phone apps since around 2007. From citizens' perspective, this constitution appears to be a one-sided political covenant, since citizens didn't sign it. But from the States' perspective, after ratification by State officers, it's the law of laws, *"...the supreme Law of the*

Land" (Article VI:2) that creates/limits the authority and scope of a federal government to **only** what's clearly written. Any authority or powers not clearly granted in writing, are denied, made clear by Amendment X. As affirmed in its breech by both Madison and Jefferson through their Virginia and Kentucky Resolutions, our federal government's legitimacy - and existence - depends upon keeping the terms of this social contract (called a "compact" in the Resolutions). And it is citizens who are supposed to hold politicians to this contract.

The Kentucky and Virginia Resolutions are wordy and florid, but they sternly affirm the constitutions' true purpose and practical effect. The main point is that any federal establishment, tax or action existing outside the authority granted in this covenant is legally null and void; no more valid than if the crazy neighbor down the street decreed it in pajamas from his Lazy Boy. And importantly, they demonstrate very well that this constitution has been under attack since the ink was wet, and those that wrote this contract were aggressive in its defense!

That defense is critically important. To understand that importance it is perhaps useful to consider the real origin of our federal constitution's key concepts and historical roots in English Common Law, and five key documents:

- The Charter of Liberties 1100
- Magna Carta Libertatum 1215
- The Petition of Right 1628
- The Grand Remonstrance 1641
- English Bill of Rights 1689

These documents and the history around them show why they failed, where everything in our constitution came from, and why Lysander Spooner was completely wrong when he wrote, *"But whether the Constitution really be one thing, or another, this much is certain - that it has either authorized such a government as we have had, or has been powerless to prevent it. In either case it is unfit to exist."*

He may as well have written, *"But whether an ignored fire extinguisher really be one thing, or another, this much is certain - that it has either authorized such fire as we have just suffered, or has been powerless to stop it. In either case it is unfit to exist."*

Constitutions are written to govern political abstractions (governments and politicians), not citizens. We failed to enforce them, as was our power and duty. Over the past generations we've voted for and even begged our politicians to stray ever more, and ever faster, from their legal boundaries. So we'd be hard-pressed to see any resemblance between our rapidly failing New Deal (old-fashioned authoritarianism), and what this Fair, Legal and Best-Ever Deal authorizes.

Here're some highlights:

- Our government-issued money is to be at least backed by gold or silver! No quasi-private Central Bank is authorized to make monopoly money.
- Most of what we call "federal" agencies, powers, laws, prohibitions, mandates and actions (including taxes, treaties and wars) are unconstitutional, and therefore legally null and void.
- State and local government should be much, much more relevant to daily life. We should scarcely detect a federal government in our lives. That was by very thoughtful design.
- There are only five federal crimes that apply to citizens.

Our ancestors knew that politics is inherently corrupting ...and violent. Nothing related to "government" happens without at least the threat of death. The IRS doesn't pass the hat and say "please;" and we could get killed by resisting an arrest for so much as a seat belt violation. Practically every political action hurts *somebody*. That is why we have constitutions ...and make politicians swear to obey them.

Politicians tend to break laws that protect us from them. This makes the laws that protect them from us null and void. But before we think any violent thoughts, remember that about 94% of us have repetitiously chosen this ungoverned government every Election Day.

The constitutions aren't perfect, but the constitutions didn't fail — we did; of our own free will. Here's to hoping we learn our lesson…

Through the following all my comments are in a box like this one. Everything else is the constitution itself. Archaic spellings like "chusing," and the punctuation and capitalization that seem odd today remain.

Some important history: In 1787 there were some, like Alexander Hamilton, who argued that the government operating under the Articles of Confederation was too weak, and that, for our survival, we needed a strong central government.[46] Not everybody agreed. The colonies had just whupped the global superpower under near-anarchy, after all. So state delegates were authorized to only **amend** the Articles. But there were two problems:

1. Under the Articles, states had to unanimously agree to any amendments. That was horribly unlikely.

2. There was at least one conspiracy afoot. In fact, it was a power grab, from the States' perspective. There were basically three opposing factions (royalists, federalists and anti-federalists), and the arguments became pretty fierce and the tactics were sneaky.

So instead of amending the Articles of Confederation, the delegates went rogue to create a new constitution. Royalists were many, some federalists were smart, and the anti-federalists were …well, they turned out to be exactly right. It's a shame they didn't win everything they wanted. But the anti-federalists won more than some would have us believe today.

All that notwithstanding, the resulting compromises, and social contract, turned out better than anybody at the time or since could've expected. Better, indeed, than any national charter before …or since.

This constitution is *still* the law of the land. The rules herein detailed are few enough that everyone can know them; simple enough that everyone can understand them; and important enough that every single one of them is to be enforced without exception, by everyone relevant, all the time.

---

[46] *"Was it not necessity which had always been the plea of every evil exertion of power, or excessive oppression? Was not necessity the pretense of every usurpation? Necessity is the plea for every infringement of human freedom. It is the argument of tyrants. It is the creed of slaves."*— William Pitt, Speech in the House of Commons, November 18, 1783

Preamble

We the People of the United States, in Order to form a more perfect
Union, establish Justice, insure domestic Tranquility, provide for the
common defence, promote the general Welfare, and secure the Blessings
of Liberty to ourselves and our Posterity, do ordain and establish this
Constitution for the United States of America.

When Gouverneur Morris wrote this preamble, he intended to elegantly
and poetically state the parties, the purpose and the action of instituting a
constitution for a new nation. And that's pretty much it. Too much has
been made of the "*We the People of the United States*" phrase. Some read it
as some presumption of communalism, as an assertion of citizen
sovereignty (closer to the fact), or as an assertion of States-as-People (it
was selected State representatives, as abstract entities, not ordinary
citizens, who signed the contract, after all). But that's mostly distraction;
this is only a Preamble. The defining laws are what follow.

Article I (The Legislative Branch)

Section 1 (Exclusive Authority)

All legislative Powers herein granted shall be vested in a Congress of the
United States, which shall consist of a Senate and House of
Representatives.

This is crucial. "*All legislative Powers herein granted shall be vested in a…*"
means that **no other** federal entity has any power to make law. IRS
"regulations" aren't law. Executive Orders are just orders of execution,
not new law. Judicial rulings and judgments are NOT law.

The one sentence of Section I nullifies most of our "federal" government,
its actions and powers. Executive bureaucracies like the FDA, IRS, EPA;
individuals like the President or a judge; and quasi-private corporations
with governing power like the "Federal Reserve" only **illegally** make
"regulations," Executive Orders or rulings with the effect of binding law.

Some have tried to excuse the phrase, *"Congress shall have power to enforce this article by appropriate legislation..."* that first appeared in Amendment XIII and popped up often thereafter, as considered necessary to prevent "judicial activism." But that's debunked by all the rest of the constitution, as well as our history and current events. Courts cannot constitutionally legislate ...and Congress can't constitutionally enforce (exclusively an executive function) anything. So, by the time the later wording appeared, the smart, wise politicians were dead, and our defense of federalism and constitutional rule of law was already fading into legalistic mush.

Section 2 (The House of Representatives)

1: The House of Representatives shall be composed of Members chosen every second Year by the People of the several States, and the Electors in each State shall have the Qualifications requisite for Electors of the most numerous Branch of the State Legislature.

This section leaves many details to the states regarding the selection of federal reps. It does specify popular elections (chosen … by "the People"), so this mention of "Electors," which in Article II or Amendment XII comprise the so-called "Electoral College," may seem a bit confusing. The founders used "electors" instead of "citizens" because there was still a debate whether only freeholders (free landowning men, at the time) could vote. This was the "stake in the game" argument that still resurfaces in many contexts today.

This same, "electors" wording, this time confusingly combined with "the people," resurfaced in Amendment 17…after it had already been settled that former slaves and non-freeholders could vote. Until the 17th, both the President and US Senators were originally to be chosen by specific State-level proxies, "electors" who were chosen by citizen voters… however defined by the states.

It has always been up to the states who can vote! Women and blacks were never denied the vote by this constitution, and indeed women could vote in New Jersey until 1807. It was only state law, not federal law that limited citizens' – or even slaves' – rights to vote.

2: No Person shall be a Representative who shall not have attained to the

Age of twenty-five Years, and been seven Years a Citizen of the United States, and who shall not, when elected, be an Inhabitant of that State in which he shall be chosen.

3: Representatives and direct Taxes shall be apportioned among the several States which may be included within this Union, according to their respective Numbers, which shall be determined by adding to the whole Number of free Persons, including those bound to Service for a Term of Years, and excluding Indians not taxed, three fifths of all other Persons.

The phrase "…*three fifths of all other Persons*" is almost always totally misunderstood. It was an attempt to reduce the disproportionate power of southern states by discounting slaves for the apportionment of US House reps. To be fairer, slaves shouldn't have been counted at all, as they certainly had no representation in government.

We are violating this principle of citizen representation today! Our census counted everybody in the USA, including illegal aliens, so states with more illegal aliens have gained disproportionate power in both Congress, and the Electoral College. States that have controlled their illegal alien population have been, in effect, penalized.

This is no statement of right or wrong, as there are merits both ways. But it is current fact.

The actual Enumeration shall be made within three Years after the first Meeting of the Congress of the United States, and within every subsequent Term of ten Years, in such Manner as they shall by Law direct. The Number of Representatives shall not exceed one for every thirty Thousand, but each State shall have at Least one Representative; and until such enumeration shall be made, the State of New Hampshire shall be entitled to chuse three, Massachusetts eight, Rhode-Island and Providence Plantations one, Connecticut five, New-York six, New Jersey four, Pennsylvania eight, Delaware one, Maryland six, Virginia ten, North Carolina five, South Carolina five, and Georgia three.

Above is the mandate for a decennial census. It's for **only** the apportionment of representatives and electors in the Electoral College. And since the number of US House Representatives was fixed at 435 based on the 1910 census by the "Permanent Apportionment Act of

1929," counting illegal aliens actually steals influence from districts that lose relative population from the non-citizen influx.

A case could be made that the founders would consider us under-represented today – averaging only one rep for ~764,161 people! There wasn't a very good reason to lock in the number of reps a hundred years ago (still not a constitutional limitation). And with fewer reps, the moneyed mighty have disproportionate power. With more reps, it'd cost more to buy them all. And maybe reps wouldn't be such celebrity/lifetime royalty icons if the districts were smaller, with less power each.

Who knows; with 5000 reps maybe we'd save enough money from less corrupt governance that the extra paychecks and a new meeting place (repurposed stadium? Or just online/virtual?) for them would seem like a bargain... More on this later.

4: When vacancies happen in the Representation from any State, the Executive Authority thereof shall issue Writs of Election to fill such Vacancies.

5: The House of Representatives shall chuse their Speaker and other Officers; and shall have the sole Power of Impeachment.

#5 does grant a lot of leeway in the devising of rules and powers within the House of Reps.

But nowhere in this constitution is any authority to grant power to anything other than human beings. This is constitutionally very important, in that political parties are non-constitutional entities (not forbidden, but not authorized in any way) that have, in effect, unconstitutional powers as if they were specially authorized people.

As already detailed in "About our 'Two-Party System'," our wiser founders warned us about political parties!

Section 3 (The Senate)

1: The Senate of the United States shall be composed of two Senators from each State, chosen by the Legislature thereof, for six Years; and each Senator shall have one Vote.

> Federal Senators were to be **directly** chosen by **state legislators** until the 17th Amendment. There were very good reasons for this.
>
> US Senators should be, in the view of our founders as well as many today, the federal defenders of the **state** constitutions and state autonomy.
>
> Notice the last phrase of Section 3:1, "…*and each Senator shall have one Vote*." I've always meant to research that…

2: Immediately after they shall be assembled in Consequence of the first Election, they shall be divided as equally as may be into three Classes. The Seats of the Senators of the first Class shall be vacated at the Expiration of the second Year, of the second Class at the Expiration of the fourth Year, and of the third Class at the Expiration of the sixth Year, so that one third may be chosen every second Year; and if Vacancies happen by Resignation, or otherwise, during the Recess of the Legislature of any State, the Executive thereof may make temporary Appointments until the next Meeting of the Legislature, which shall then fill such Vacancies.

3: No Person shall be a Senator who shall not have attained to the Age of thirty Years, and been nine Years a Citizen of the United States, and who shall not, when elected, be an Inhabitant of that State for which he shall be chosen.

4: The Vice President of the United States shall be President of the Senate, but shall have no Vote, unless they be equally divided.

5: The Senate shall chuse their other Officers, and also a President pro tempore, in the Absence of the Vice President, or when he shall exercise the Office of President of the United States.

6: The Senate shall have the sole Power to try all Impeachments. When sitting for that Purpose, they shall be on Oath or Affirmation. When the President of the United States is tried, the Chief Justice shall preside: And no Person shall be convicted without the Concurrence of two thirds of the Members present.

7: Judgment in Cases of impeachment shall not extend further than to removal from Office, and disqualification to hold and enjoy any Office of honor, Trust or Profit under the United States: but the Party convicted shall nevertheless be liable and subject to Indictment, Trial, Judgment and Punishment, according to Law.

OK, trick question – who currently leads the senate? Many have been led to believe that the US Senate Majority Leader (a non-constitutional and inherently divisive partisan office) presides over the senate.

But the Vice-President is the President of the US Senate! (Section 3.4 above)

The only time the VP is not to preside, in fact, is when either acting as President of the USA, or when the President is being impeached. Interestingly, it's already been brought up by the comically corrupt VP Spiro Agnew that the VP could preside over his own impeachment!

The VP of the USA is **not an assistant President!** This is a powerful position, intended to *counter* the power of the President from the most powerful branch...the legislature. Originally, they were intended to be more adversaries than allies, because that's how they were supposed to be elected.

Constitutional design has been destroyed in favor of partisan cronyism that our founders warned against often and vigorously.

The other procedural details were given attention here because our founders assumed that impeachment would be an important occasional cleansing, and the details reflect their intentions of division and separation of powers, and firm limitation of same. It is high time to bring back the impeachment mentality with an urgent sense of purpose.

Section 4 (Meeting Times and Places)

1: The Times, Places and Manner of holding Elections for Senators and Representatives, shall be prescribed in each State by the Legislature thereof; but the Congress may at any time by Law make or alter such Regulations, except as to the Places of chusing Senators.

2: The Congress shall assemble at least once in every Year, and such Meeting shall be on the first Monday in December, unless they shall by Law appoint a different Day.

Here's more proof that our government had gone stupid by the time of Amendment XX. They didn't have to go through amendment to change meeting days; they could have simply written legislation. It says so here. But they went through the trouble of amendment …and to the amendment added, "…*unless they shall by law appoint a different day.*" …What **were** they **thinking**!? I'm thinking they never read Article I, Section 4.2.

Section 5 (Internal Rules)

1: Each House shall be the Judge of the Elections, Returns and Qualifications of its own Members, and a Majority of each shall constitute a Quorum to do Business; but a smaller Number may adjourn from day to day, and may be authorized to compel the Attendance of absent Members, in such Manner, and under such Penalties as each House may provide.

2: Each House may determine the Rules of its Proceedings, punish its Members for disorderly Behaviour, and, with the Concurrence of two thirds, expel a Member.

The self-policing powers have obviously proven to be next to worthless. Would your boss let you show up the equivalent of less than 1 day a week? Could *we* get away with insider trading and taking lavish trips on the company card? Could *we* use company stationary to apply for other jobs, or to solicit personal donations? All this and much worse happens within a Good Ol' Boy network today.

3: Each House shall keep a Journal of its Proceedings, and from time to time publish the same, excepting such Parts as may in their Judgment require Secrecy; and the Yeas and Nays of the Members of either House on any question shall, at the Desire of one fifth of those Present, be entered on the Journal.

4: Neither House, during the Session of Congress, shall, without the Consent of the other, adjourn for more than three days, nor to any other Place than that in which the two Houses shall be sitting.

> We have obvious problems with secrecy. But the secrecy mentioned here is not the most problematic. And given today's technology and the possibility of securely working remotely, it's regrettable that item 4 specifies physical location.

Section 6 (Pay, Conflict of Interest)

1: The Senators and Representatives shall receive a Compensation for their Services, to be ascertained by Law, and paid out of the Treasury of the United States. They shall in all Cases, except Treason, Felony and Breach of the Peace, be privileged from Arrest during their Attendance at the Session of their respective Houses, and in going to and returning from the same; and for any Speech or Debate in either House, they shall not be questioned in any other Place.

2: No Senator or Representative shall, during the Time for which he was elected, be appointed to any civil Office under the Authority of the United States, which shall have been created, or the Emoluments whereof shall have been encreased during such time; and no Person holding any Office under the United States, shall be a Member of either House during his Continuance in Office.

> This is a terrible problem in, for example, Indiana's part-time legislature, where teachers, police and lawyers, keeping their political employee jobs while also in political authority roles. This makes them doubly taxpayer-supported, and with unfair power over the domain of their "day job."
>
> But at the federal level, the perky pay and benefits, combined with distance, unaccountability, and the unlikelihood of ever wanting a second

job, make this a lesser problem. However, the revolving door between political office, and banks, universities or other politics-intensive businesses, demonstrates that the founders didn't close all the loopholes in their quest to leash these double-dipping, two-faced sharks among us. In fact, **insider trading is** *allowed* for congress-critters! That's just one way our politicians go in as zero-savings low-wage earners and come out as millionaires. **Corruption** is a ***catastrophic problem.***

Section 7 (Bicameral Rules)

1: All Bills for raising Revenue shall originate in the House of Representatives; but the Senate may propose or concur with Amendments as on other Bills.

2: Every Bill which shall have passed the House of Representatives and the Senate, shall, before it become a Law, be presented to the President of the United States; If he approve he shall sign it, but if not he shall return it, with his Objections to that House in which it shall have originated, who shall enter the Objections at large on their Journal, and proceed to reconsider it. If after such Reconsideration two thirds of that House shall agree to pass the Bill, it shall be sent, together with the Objections, to the other House, by which it shall likewise be reconsidered, and if approved by two thirds of that House, it shall become a Law. But in all such Cases the Votes of both Houses shall be determined by yeas and Nays, and the Names of the Persons voting for and against the Bill shall be entered on the Journal of each House respectively. If any Bill shall not be returned by the President within ten Days (Sundays excepted) after it shall have been presented to him, the Same shall be a Law, in like Manner as if he had signed it, unless the Congress by their Adjournment prevent its Return, in which Case it shall not be a Law.

3: Every Order, Resolution, or Vote to which the Concurrence of the Senate and House of Representatives may be necessary (except on a question of Adjournment) shall be presented to the President of the United States; and before the Same shall take Effect, shall be approved by him, or being disapproved by him, shall be repassed by two thirds of the Senate and House of Representatives, according to the Rules and

Limitations prescribed in the Case of a Bill.

> The preceding rules are almost the only part of this constitution that are considered sacrosanct today. So little need be said about it other than now's a fair time to point out that the constant reference to only the male gender is obviously outdated. But…
>
> **Pay close attention to the following section.** It delimits the authority of Congress. If it isn't written in plain English here or in later amendments, it is **forbidden**, as clarified by the Tenth Amendment:

Section 8 (Legislative Authority)

1: The Congress shall have Power To lay and collect Taxes, Duties, Imposts and Excises, to pay the Debts and provide for the common Defence and general Welfare of the United States; but all Duties, Imposts and Excises shall be uniform throughout the United States;

> The above "general Welfare" is where there's trouble (not from the same phrase in the Preamble). This really **does** authorize Congress to "provide for the…general Welfare of the United States." This wording is problematic for those who'd argue that "welfare programs" are entirely, inherently unconstitutional. The phrase was clearly troublesome from the start:
>
> James Madison said: "With respect to the words general welfare, I have always regarded them as qualified by the detail of powers connected with them. To take them in a literal and unlimited sense would be a metamorphosis of the Constitution into a character which there is a host of proofs was not contemplated by its creators."
>
> But the greatest limitation of this phrase is in federalism itself. The federal government has no authority at all over **citizens'** daily life; the phrase "…*of the United States*" as opposed to "…*of the People*," is key. As you'll see again in Amendment X, States and People are different entities!
>
> The federal government's jurisdiction is over the union as defined throughout this contract. The only power the feds have over individuals is in authority to tax, to punish violation of federal crimes (of which there are only five!), or over what happens in federal lands or international waters. This is an important, defining characteristic of our republic.

One early, seemingly benign stretch of this jurisdiction was the 1798 law, "An Act for the Relief of Sick and Disabled Seamen" which initially applied to only those operating on the open seas (outside of state jurisdiction, and in federal jurisdiction). It started as (deep breath) a mandatory health-insurance scheme (!), but it eventually crept into the general budget. It was, in fact, socialized healthcare! And it grew, as all government things do, into what is now the Public Health Service.

2: To borrow Money on the credit of the United States;

Yes, a national debt **is** constitutional! But **for *what*** is debt authorized? Aye, there's the rub. Most of what is **spent** is unconstitutional. Read on…

3: To regulate Commerce with foreign Nations, and among the several States, and with the Indian Tribes;

There's no denying from the wording here that the federal government has jurisdiction over trade issues **between** states (among seems like an odd word choice based on its use today). In the context of regulating trade "***with*** *foreign Nations*" and "***with*** *Indian Tribes*" some now argue that the feds have authority over **all** trade **within** states. That would mean, of course, that congress could, by legislation, regulate all trade worldwide! Until FDR's "New Deal" (a bad deal if ever there was one – and crazy too – look up the SCOTUS decision in *Wickard v. Filburn*!), nobody tried to "interpret" this law in any way other than to handle disputes between states. Even trade with foreign nations and native tribes was for decades remarkably free of any federal involvement. In general, these author's comments (and Madison's) from Section 8:1 apply here.

So the feds have no authority over any commerce that takes place entirely within a state. This also is a defining characteristic of our republic, and of its delineations and limitation of law and jurisdiction. Goods made in Indiana and sold in Indiana should be free of any federal regulation, given the scope of federal powers and citizen rights defined elsewhere in this contract.

Of course, Amendment XVIII modified this; alcohol was a prohibited product in every state by legitimate, constitutionally authorized federal law. **But the amendment was repealed, and nothing similar has replaced it.**

I'm not saying that there isn't room for debate, and this "Commerce Clause" should be severely restricted by amendment. But this "Commerce Clause" has been stretched so far beyond what's legitimate (and sane) that the violations and usurpations are now surreal…and destructive.

4: To establish an uniform Rule of Naturalization, and uniform Laws on the subject of Bankruptcies throughout the United States;

OK, so "…*an uniform Rule of Naturalization*" has been established, though it's not uniformly enforced. But where in this contract is any federal authority to usurp States' internal rights and laws regarding borders, citizenship and state-funded privileges? For another take on current events, read the constitutions of Arizona or Texas to see just how much voters have allowed the feds to fib, and fail us, in a key responsibility.

5: To coin Money, regulate the Value thereof, and of foreign Coin, and fix the Standard of Weights and Measures;

Here, ironically, sadly and criminally, the feds do not exert the full measure of their authority. They've left certain key issues of weights and measures (like time zones) up to the states, or private industry (which has largely gone metric). Much worse, however, *they've delegated away their power over money* (now just paper debt coupons) to private, and often foreign, banker/ moneychangers. This is where our founders specifically made paper fiat currency unconstitutional.

6: To provide for the Punishment of counterfeiting the Securities and current Coin of the United States;

OK, here's one federal crime that applies to citizens; counterfeiting.

It applies to the Fed, too… The Fed should be ended, and those involved in the fraud and counterfeiting should be punished. But, as we should've learned from past and current history, the people behind this will do anything to protect their cabal's racket.

7: To establish Post Offices and post Roads;

Notice that only "…*post Roads*" are authorized. All other roads, canals (and starting in the 1820's, railways), were in private or state jurisdictions.

Indiana, for example, went broke with canal building, though it was forbidden by the Indiana Constitution of 1816.

The true history of roads and railways is that the best quality, lowest cost, fastest innovation occurred in private hands. That this made some people rich while everybody else benefited, wasn't a problem.

8: To promote the Progress of Science and useful Arts, by securing for limited Times to Authors and Inventors the exclusive Right to their respective Writings and Discoveries;

9: To constitute Tribunals inferior to the supreme Court;

10: To define and punish Piracies and Felonies committed on the high Seas, and Offences against the Law of Nations;

Above are federal crimes #s 2 through 4 a citizen could commit: piracy, high seas felony, and offense against the Law of Nations. It's debatable what "Felonies committed on the high Seas" entails only because we've greatly warped the meaning of "felony" since the Prohibition Era. But note that it doesn't grant authority over felonies on land, which would be under other jurisdictions (e.g., States). At the time it was written, "*Felonies*" meant serious crimes (crimes violate actual victims; offenses violate only laws) committed at sea. Presumably, we should amend this to include air space today.

"*Offences against the Law of Nations*" is very abstract and wide-open. The theory behind the law of nations (*jus gentium*) is a lofty presumption that all sovereign states can share a basis of civility according to treaties, customs and general principles of justice. But this theoretical sketch of a hazy outline creates an opening by which nefarious foreigners (or, for the past 90 years, apparently, American leaders) can twist our laws against us.

11: To declare War, grant Letters of Marque and Reprisal, and make Rules concerning Captures on Land and Water;

This is a pretty big deal. We've had scarcely a year's peace since the War to End All Wars, but there's not been a constitutionally declared war since WWII! This makes laws related to war moot; hence so many legal, let alone moral issues related to Blackwater /Xe/ Academi, Guantanamo Bay, "terrorism," etc.

The so-called "War on Terror" could have been handled through Letters of Marque and Reprisal (authorized violence and confiscation …whether that is sensible is another subject) against specific people/groups, since no official government has been named an enemy lately. But Congress dodged this responsibility and gave it to the President. That's both foolish, and illegal. And illegal war is…what, exactly?

12: To raise and support Armies, but no Appropriation of Money to that Use shall be for a longer Term than two Years;

Some try to argue that the founders weren't concerned about permanent, professional armies; but that's bizarre, and contradicted by the founders' own words. While they did allow for short term funding of a standing army, it was short-term to ensure that the federal army was never any threat to the state militias! State militias had separate funding, training and maintenance authorizations **without** term limits. The only permanent armed forces our founders intended were the militia, and the navy (because ships were expensive and required upkeep…analogous to modern aircraft and space vehicles). The following provision of the Navy could be amended to cover more modern costly armaments inherently dedicated to trans-border disputes (bombers, ICBMs, etc.) But the founders were very clear in their fear of permanent national armed forces dependent upon transnational conflict…or oppression… for their livelihoods.

13: To provide and maintain a Navy;

14: To make Rules for the Government and Regulation of the land and naval Forces;

So state militias must conform to national standards. OK, fine.

15: To provide for calling forth the Militia to execute the Laws of the Union, suppress Insurrections and repel Invasions;

This really does authorize the federal government, if it's acting constitutionally from its side of the fence, to use violence against our own citizens as well as foreigners who violate federal laws, or incite the hard-to-define trouble called "Insurrections." So for those who claim that armed rebellion is a right, or even that states have a right to secede, this

16: To provide for organizing, arming, and disciplining, the Militia, and for governing such Part of them as may be employed in the Service of the United States, reserving to the States respectively, the Appointment of the Officers, and the Authority of training the Militia according to the discipline prescribed by Congress;

No amendment changed what's above. Whether we like it or not, it is still the law that militias are State forces. When no properly declared state of war exists, the Indiana Militia (just for example) is under their state Commander in Chief – the Governor of Indiana. (Art. 12, sec. 2 of the Indiana Constitution…even after the 1974 amendments!) Only when – and for only as long as – Congress calls forth the militias by declaration of war, are they "federal" armed forces.

The "Militia Act of 1903," or the so-called "Dick Act" should've been annulled long ago, as it was an anti-constitutional establishment of a permanent, transnational war machine that essentially destroyed the militia system. But in law, the militia still exist...

17: To exercise exclusive Legislation in all Cases whatsoever, over such District (not exceeding ten Miles square) as may, by Cession of particular States, and the Acceptance of Congress, become the Seat of the Government of the United States, and to exercise like Authority over all Places purchased by the Consent of the Legislature of the State in which the Same shall be, for the Erection of Forts, Magazines, Arsenals, dock-Yards, and other needful Buildings;--And

18: To make all Laws which shall be necessary and proper for carrying into Execution the foregoing Powers, and all other Powers vested by this Constitution in the Government of the United States, or in any Department or Officer thereof.

This created Washington, D.C., and provided the sole authority for Congress, not local politicians, to make law, as well as delimit the creation and powers of federal government over federal land as agreeable to the states. This authority doesn't exist over any other square inch in any

State.
This creates a small seat of federal power...***not*** a *state!* It has obviously
been a mistake to grant such a hotbed of corruption and political
inbreeding home rule. It'd be a catastrophe to make it a state.

Section 9 (Enumerated Limitations)

1: The Migration or Importation of such Persons as any of the States now
existing shall think proper to admit, shall not be prohibited by the
Congress prior to the Year one thousand eight hundred and eight, but a
Tax or duty may be imposed on such Importation, not exceeding ten
dollars for each Person.

2: The Privilege of the Writ of Habeas Corpus shall not be suspended,
unless when in Cases of Rebellion or Invasion the public Safety may
require it.

We should strike the last phrase from the above. When Habeas Corpus
was suspended (by Presidents Lincoln and GW Bush) it was a painful
travesty that did no good at all. And of course it's embarrassing that 9.1
didn't prohibit slavery. But the constitution would never have never
become law with that prohibition at that time.

3: No Bill of Attainder or ex post facto Law shall be passed.

A "Bill of Attainder" is legislation that specifically calls out an individual
or group as, literally, tainted; and essentially judges and punishes without a
trial. This was mostly written to reinforce the separation of powers;
legislators are herewith prevented judicial/executive powers. Most
obvious violations of this principle were not actually committed by
Congress. It's been Executive and bureaucratic actions (like the
FBI/FDR's 1939 Custodial Detention Index that was used for the
internment of Japanese, Italian and German citizens) that've been the
worst violations of this.

But as with England's "bills of pains and penalties," which included
special taxation/fees that could be applied to disfavored groups like
churches or sects, our corporate laws (many written for/against specific

corporations/ unions/ churches) and tax rates are legislative branch violations.

More common than such punishments, however, are specially favored, and of course unconstitutional treatments under law. One notable and egregious example is the previously mentioned National Childhood Vaccine Injury Act of 1986, which transfers accountability for harm caused by vaccines from vaccine manufacturers, to taxpayers, and creates a wall of immunity and unaccountability for only this one industry.

An ex post facto law is a retroactive law. Some argue that some laws and practices like "three strikes" or certain sex-offender laws violate this. Many tax regulations have retroactive implications, and are of course, violations of this constitution.

4: No Capitation, or other direct, Tax shall be laid, unless in Proportion to the Census or Enumeration herein before directed to be taken.

Amendment XVI killed off this reasonable limitation and instituted, instead, our genuinely evil and destructive income tax.

5: No Tax or Duty shall be laid on Articles exported from any State.

6: No Preference shall be given by any Regulation of Commerce or Revenue to the Ports of one State over those of another: nor shall Vessels bound to, or from, one State, be obliged to enter, clear, or pay Duties in another.

7: No Money shall be drawn from the Treasury, but in Consequence of Appropriations made by Law; and a regular Statement and Account of the Receipts and Expenditures of all public Money shall be published from time to time.

This one's been stretched and pulled like toffee. The previous chapter about The Fed scarcely touched the laundering between "The Fed" and the Treasury, but there are many more in-depth books and articles on this subject. And what happens additionally with "security" and (euphemistically) "intelligence" "off books" spending is appalling.

8: No Title of Nobility shall be granted by the United States: And no Person holding any Office of Profit or Trust under them, shall, without the Consent of the Congress, accept of any present, Emolument, Office, or Title, of any kind whatever, from any King, Prince, or foreign State.

> This **includes** titles like "The Honorable…" and "Esquire." If we were to clean out our titled nobility, there'd be only beggars and museum curators left in DC. And, fortunately, we're starting to finally get confirmation that many of our politicians have not just recently, but for some time, been accepting foreign money in exchange for foreign influence.

> **Pay close attention to the following section**, as it encompasses the limitations placed on states within the union. No other limitations on citizens or states exist other than what's constitutionally delegated to the federal authority and denied state authority in the following section.

Section 10 (State Limitations)

1: No State shall enter into any Treaty, Alliance, or Confederation; grant Letters of Marque and Reprisal; coin Money; emit Bills of Credit; make any Thing but gold and silver Coin a Tender in Payment of Debts; pass any Bill of Attainder, ex post facto Law, or Law impairing the Obligation of Contracts, or grant any Title of Nobility.

> In the context of The Fed's monetary mayhem since 1913, this phrase, "*…coin Money; emit Bills of Credit; make any Thing but gold and silver Coin a Tender in Payment of Debts*," may be the most ominously impactful group of words in the constitution. The states, as well as the budding nation's previous "national" governments, had been issuing unbacked paper bills of credit and other forms of funny money to already disastrous effects. So the constitution's authors made certain to forbid such fiat currency swindles and hidden taxes in the future.
>
> Unfortunately, we've allowed unconstitutional central banking, which has catastrophically doomed our economy to the trifecta of boom/bust cycles, the theft described by the Cantillon Effect, and the eventual monetary collapse described by the Triffin Paradox. And it looks like proposals for digital currency will only make all this even more dystopian…if we don't wake up and restore sound money.

2: No State shall, without the Consent of the Congress, lay any Imposts or
Duties on Imports or Exports, except what may be absolutely necessary
for executing its inspection Laws: and the net Produce of all Duties and
Imposts, laid by any State on Imports or Exports, shall be for the Use of
the Treasury of the United States; and all such Laws shall be subject to the
Revision and Controul of the Congress.

3: No State shall, without the Consent of Congress, lay any Duty of
Tonnage, keep Troops, or Ships of War in time of Peace, enter into any
Agreement or Compact with another State, or with a foreign Power, or
engage in War, unless actually invaded, or in such imminent Danger as
will not admit of delay.

> Governors and Secretaries of State are always traveling these days to enter
> "Agreement or Compact with another State, or with a foreign Power."
> But otherwise, the states have stayed limited as described above. Worse,
> though, is that illegal alien invasion (to an astounding scale) happens
> without any state action, which is clearly in their jurisdiction.
>
> Incidentally, the "keep Troops" prohibition referred to permanent paid,
> or standing, armies. Another clue that standing armies (that depend upon
> aggression for their relevance, and to earn their keep) were considered a
> bad thing, while a citizen militia (that'd rather tend to business and home)
> was considered the cure.

Article II (The Executive Branch)

Section 1 (Exclusive Authority, Term and Election)

1: The executive Power shall be vested in a President of the United States of America. He shall hold his Office during the Term of four Years, and, together with the Vice President, chosen for the same Term, be elected, as follows.

> Section 1 of the first three Articles makes plain the separation and exclusivity of powers. Only legislators may legislate. Only executives may execute. Only judges may judge.

2: Each State shall appoint, in such Manner as the Legislature thereof may direct, a Number of Electors, equal to the whole Number of Senators and Representatives to which the State may be entitled in the Congress: but no Senator or Representative, or Person holding an Office of Trust or Profit under the United States, shall be appointed an Elector.

3: The Electors shall meet in their respective States, and vote by Ballot for two Persons, of whom one at least shall not be an Inhabitant of the same State with themselves. And they shall make a List of all the Persons voted for, and of the Number of Votes for each; which List they shall sign and certify, and transmit sealed to the Seat of the Government of the United States, directed to the President of the Senate. The President of the Senate shall, in the Presence of the Senate and House of Representatives, open all the Certificates, and the Votes shall then be counted.

> The number of electors is very important, which makes the census very important. And electors must vote for at least one candidate (either POTUS or VPOTUS – remember, this wasn't a combined ticket back then) who isn't a resident of their own state, to minimize state bias.
>
> Questions: Was this supposed to be a merely clerical role for the Senate? Is there implied authority to question the States' electors should there be questions of fraud? Was Mike Pence constitutionally correct to reject any such contest in the 2020 Election? See Amendment 12 – the POTUS/VPOTUS election is determined in the Senate.
>
> And from the wording of the previous, isn't it obvious that political parties were to be no part of their deliberations?

The Person having the greatest Number of Votes shall be the President, if such Number be a Majority of the whole Number of Electors appointed; and if there be more than one who have such Majority, and have an equal Number of Votes, then the House of Representatives shall immediately chuse by Ballot one of them for President; and if no Person have a Majority, then from the five highest on the List the said House shall in like Manner chuse the President. But in chusing the President, the Votes shall be taken by States, the Representation from each State having one Vote; A quorum for this Purpose shall consist of a Member or Members from two thirds of the States, and a Majority of all the States shall be necessary to a Choice. In every Case, after the Choice of the President, the Person having the greatest Number of Votes of the Electors shall be the Vice President. But if there should remain two or more who have equal Votes, the Senate shall chuse from them by Ballot the Vice President.

We don't elect the VP this way of course, though the Electors (Electoral College) really do choose the POTUS and VP; it's not by our popular vote. Amendment XII doesn't legitimize the bizarre democratic/electoral college hybrid by which we elect Presidents today. We should fix this…after electing better politicians who'd fix this instead of making it worse, obviously.

We've come to mistrust the Electoral College system today mostly because:
1. Most of us don't understand it.
2. The two entrenched parties have taken over the whole system and corrupted it.
3. We can no longer directly choose the electors as we're supposed to. *THAT* is a big deal!

And did you notice the wording, "…the *five* highest on the List?" Not just two?

Just imagine how different our elections would be if we'd all consider more options, and reduce the power of parties.

4: The Congress may determine the Time of chusing the Electors, and the Day on which they shall give their Votes; which Day shall be the same throughout the United States.

5: No Person except a natural born Citizen, or a Citizen of the United States, at the time of the Adoption of this Constitution, shall be eligible to the Office of President; neither shall any Person be eligible to that Office who shall not have attained to the Age of thirty-five Years, and been fourteen Years a Resident within the United States.

> There's been much misdirection over the "natural born" clause, while too much of the rest of the constitution, in scope and detail, has been ignored.
>
> The words, "natural born" did have special meaning to the founders' definition of a republic, but this, and the nature of republican rights, roles and definitions is best described in another book. I recommend "America's Republican Form of Government" by Kurt St. Angelo.

6: In Case of the Removal of the President from Office, or of his Death, Resignation, or Inability to discharge the Powers and Duties of the said Office, the Same shall devolve on the Vice President, and the Congress may by Law provide for the Case of Removal, Death, Resignation or Inability, both of the President and Vice President, declaring what Officer shall then act as President, and such Officer shall act accordingly, until the Disability be removed, or a President shall be elected.

> Read the preceding very carefully, and tell me exactly why we needed Amendment XXV. Congress is hereby granted the authority to decide succession by legislation. No amendment was necessary, as the authority was already granted.

7: The President shall, at stated Times, receive for his Services, a Compensation, which shall neither be encreased nor diminished during the Period for which he shall have been elected, and he shall not receive within that Period any other Emolument from the United States, or any of them.

8: Before he enter on the Execution of his Office, he shall take the following Oath or Affirmation:--"I do solemnly swear (or affirm) that I will faithfully execute the Office of President of the United States, and will to the best of my Ability, preserve, protect and defend the Constitution of the United States."

The preceding oath/affirmation is at least equivalent to signing the contract. The greater the power, the greater the responsibility…and the USA President is accountable to the enforcement of the USA Constitution, as written. It's his job to enforce it. This says so.

Section 2 (Executive Authority)

1: The President shall be Commander in Chief of the Army and Navy of the United States, and of the Militia of the several States, when called into the actual Service of the United States; he may require the Opinion, in writing, of the principal Officer in each of the executive Departments, upon any Subject relating to the Duties of their respective Offices, and he shall have Power to grant Reprieves and Pardons for Offences against the United States, except in Cases of Impeachment.

Don't miss this: "The President shall be Commander in Chief … **when** called into the actual Service of the United States." This is the active phrase – "…when called into the **actual** Service…" Here, again, it is clear that he's the CIC of the militias **only** under a constitutional declaration of war. And there hasn't been such a declaration since WWII.

2: He shall have Power, by and with the Advice and Consent of the Senate, to make Treaties, provided two thirds of the Senators present concur; and he shall nominate, and by and with the Advice and Consent of the Senate, shall appoint Ambassadors, other public Ministers and Consuls, Judges of the supreme Court, and all other Officers of the United States, whose Appointments are not herein otherwise provided for, and which shall be established by Law: but the Congress may by Law vest the Appointment of such inferior Officers, as they think proper, in the President alone, in the Courts of Law, or in the Heads of Departments.

Just because the President can appoint *"other Officers of the United States, whose Appointments are not herein otherwise provided for"* does not mean that those officers somehow gain powers that aren't specifically authorized by this constitution. In fact, there is no federal authority beyond what's authored here. So we'd have to amend the constitution to legitimize today's three-branch powers of the EPA, IRS, FBI, etc., etc., et cetera.

One power that, for the nefarious and foolish, offers an easy path to overthrowing the constitution, is the power of making treaties. It is constitutional, though self-destructive, to make treaties that cede *constitutional* authority to foreigners (see Article VI, Sect.2). It has been done, and it's being done now. However, a legitimate treaty is an agreement between political states, not people. Those who wrote this law knew this to mean that treaties could not exceed the authority of states, and were of course, in no way, a controlling authority over the normal activity of citizens. Only in matters of transnational trade or travel could a legitimate treaty affect ordinary citizens.

The controlling justice here is that you can't give away what's not yours. The federal government cannot give away what it does not own. And most treaties and international agreements today, exemplified lately by the world's self-immolating response to COVID-19, granting political authority to pharmaceutical companies and a few unelected public health bureaucrats, are unconstitutional power grabs.

Many of what we now call treaties are not treaties at all. They are transnational legislative, judicial and executive decrees that have no more legitimacy than if that crazy neighbor down the street declared himself ruler of the world. That includes the UN's "non-binding" but seemingly almighty Agenda 21.

3: The President shall have Power to fill up all Vacancies that may happen during the Recess of the Senate, by granting Commissions which shall expire at the End of their next Session.

Section 3 (Enforce the Laws)

He shall from time to time give to the Congress Information of the State of the Union, and recommend to their Consideration such Measures as he shall judge necessary and expedient; he may, on extraordinary Occasions, convene both Houses, or either of them, and in Case of Disagreement between them, with Respect to the Time of Adjournment, he may adjourn them to such Time as he shall think proper; he shall receive Ambassadors and other public Ministers; he shall take Care that the Laws be faithfully executed, and shall Commission all the Officers of the United States.

> **THIS, and only this, is the *authority* of Executive Orders.** A constitutional, legal EO decrees the details, procedure and method of enforcing laws written by legislators. This single, admittedly run-on sentence also contains the limits of executive agencies, which can act only upon legislation written by legislators, judgments made by judges, and execution ordered by the executive officeholder.

Section 4 (Removal from Office)

The President, Vice President and all civil Officers of the United States, shall be removed from Office on Impeachment for, and Conviction of, Treason, Bribery, or other high Crimes and Misdemeanors.

> Violating the oath of office by violating this critical social contract is more than just a misdemeanor. It can be treason. But at the very least, we could remove most politicians currently in office with this section.
>
> But they're there because We The People put them there.

Article III (The Judicial Branch)
Section 1 (Exclusive Authority)

The judicial Power of the United States, shall be vested in one supreme Court, and in such inferior Courts as the Congress may from time to time ordain and establish. The Judges, both of the supreme and inferior Courts, shall hold their Offices during good Behaviour, and shall, at stated Times, receive for their Services, a Compensation, which shall not be diminished during their Continuance in Office.

> Just a reminder…this authorizes **judicial** powers *only*. No legislative or executive powers at all. Here's what even the "big government" elitist among the founders, Alexander Hamilton, said about this in Federalist #78: *"The judiciary, on the contrary, has no influence over either the sword or the purse; no direction either of the strength or of the wealth of the society; and can take no active resolution whatever. It may truly be said to have neither FORCE nor WILL, but merely judgment; and must ultimately depend upon the aid of the executive arm even for the efficacy of its judgments."*

Section 2 (Judicial Power)

1: The judicial Power shall extend to all Cases, in Law and Equity, arising under this Constitution, the Laws of the United States, and Treaties made, or which shall be made, under their Authority;--to all Cases affecting Ambassadors, other public Ministers and Consuls;--to all Cases of admiralty and maritime Jurisdiction;--to Controversies to which the United States shall be a Party;--to Controversies between two or more States;--between a State and Citizens of another State; -between Citizens of different States, --between Citizens of the same State claiming Lands under Grants of different States, and between a State, or the Citizens thereof, and foreign States, Citizens or Subjects.

> Amendment XI actually narrows the jurisdiction of the courts from what's authorized above. And what's authorized is very specifically "under this Constitution," and not to be deferred to the other legitimate branches of government, and certainly not to our unelected, vast and powerful bureaucracy. Yet now, and even worse since the 1985 *Chevron v.*

2: In all Cases affecting Ambassadors, other public Ministers and Consuls, and those in which a State shall be Party, the supreme Court shall have original Jurisdiction. In all the other Cases before mentioned, the supreme Court shall have appellate Jurisdiction, both as to Law and Fact, with such Exceptions, and under such Regulations as the Congress shall make.

3: The Trial of all Crimes, except in Cases of Impeachment, shall be by Jury; and such Trial shall be held in the State where the said Crimes shall have been committed; but when not committed within any State, the Trial shall be at such Place or Places as the Congress may by Law have directed.

Section 3 (Treason)

1: Treason against the United States, shall consist only in levying War against them, or in adhering to their Enemies, giving them Aid and Comfort. No Person shall be convicted of Treason unless on the Testimony of two Witnesses to the same overt Act, or on Confession in open Court.

2: The Congress shall have Power to declare the Punishment of Treason, but no Attainder of Treason shall work Corruption of Blood, or Forfeiture except during the Life of the Person attainted.

Article IV (States)

Section 1 (Uniform Applicability)

Full Faith and Credit shall be given in each State to the public Acts, Records, and judicial Proceedings of every other State. And the Congress may by general Laws prescribe the Manner in which such Acts, Records and Proceedings shall be proved, and the Effect thereof.

So, constitutionally (don't shoot the messenger...) if a state decides that gay marriage, or polygamy, or contractual arrangements with other species are legitimate, then Congress already has the authority to decide how this is to work throughout the union. No amendment is necessary.

Don't confuse this with the "gay marriage" debate in detail, however, since most of what that now entails is about fair/equal application of Social Security, employment, visitation, bereavement pay, property, medical and inheritance rules. Churches gave marriage unto Caesar generations ago[47], and there should be no surprise at what Caesar did to the institution.

Section 2 (Citizen Rights)

1: The Citizens of each State shall be entitled to all Privileges and Immunities of Citizens in the several States.

This affirms the expansive, infinite power of rights, and the narrow, finite nature of legitimate political authority.

2: A Person charged in any State with Treason, Felony, or other Crime, who shall flee from Justice, and be found in another State, shall on Demand of the executive Authority of the State from

---

[47] Ministers say of their own free will, "By the power vested in me by the State of…" They're not invoking God's Will; they've summoned Caesar.

which he fled, be delivered up, to be removed to the State having
Jurisdiction of the Crime.

3: No Person held to Service or Labour in one State, under the
Laws thereof, escaping into another, shall, in Consequence of any
Law or Regulation therein, be discharged from such Service or
Labour, but shall be delivered up on Claim of the Party to whom
such Service or Labour may be due.

Section 3 (Jurisdiction and Statehood)

1: New States may be admitted by the Congress into this Union;
but no new State shall be formed or erected within the Jurisdiction
of any other State; nor any State be formed by the Junction of two
or more States, or Parts of States, without the Consent of the
Legislatures of the States concerned as well as of the Congress.

2: The Congress shall have Power to dispose of and make all
needful Rules and Regulations respecting the Territory or other
Property belonging to the United States; and nothing in this
Constitution shall be so construed as to Prejudice any Claims of the

United States, or of any particular State.

> What constitutes constitutional "Property belonging to the United States?" This is beyond the scope of these annotations, but beyond those early acquisitions (Louisiana Purchase, for example), Washington, D.C., and lands deeded in trust (typically parklands, and typically deeded in perpetuity), the federal government should not "own" very much at all.

Section 4 (Republican Government)

The United States shall guarantee to every State in this Union a Republican Form of Government, and shall protect each of them against Invasion; and on Application of the Legislature, or of the Executive (when the Legislature cannot be convened) against domestic Violence.

> Of course, *"Republican Form of Government"* does not mean GOP forever! Republican means government by proxy, or representatives chosen under the assumption that citizens retain all power, and can replace those proxies on Election Day. It's a theoretical form, actually; republican representatives eventually become despots when "the people" lose their will and wits…as we apparently have.
>
> Also, when the feds **don't** protect States against invasion, the states have an already enumerated right to self-protection (Article I, Sec. 10:3). And please don't confuse our current notions of "domestic violence" with this "domestic Violence," which is about insurrection.

Article V (Amendment Process)

The Congress, whenever two thirds of both Houses shall deem it necessary, shall propose Amendments to this Constitution, or, on the Application of the Legislatures of two thirds of the several States, shall call a Convention for proposing Amendments, which, in either Case, shall be valid to all Intents and Purposes, as Part of this Constitution, when ratified by the Legislatures of three fourths of the several States, or by Conventions in three fourths thereof, as the one or the other Mode of Ratification may be proposed by the Congress; Provided that no Amendment which may be made prior to the Year One thousand eight hundred and eight shall in any Manner affect the first and fourth Clauses in the Ninth Section of the first Article; and that no State, without its Consent, shall be deprived of its equal Suffrage in the Senate.

> It's supposed to be hard to amend this contract. It shouldn't be undertaken thoughtlessly or with poor punctuation and grammar. Some amendments were both necessary and well-done. …Others? Sigh…
>
> But this is the state authority cited by COS (Convention of States) and "Article V Convention" proponents for changing the constitution. The authority is there, but the implication that the constitution is what needs changing is dangerously incorrect, and a terrible copout. The constitution isn't what's messing up our country. No, We The People are doing that all by ourselves.

Article VI (Legal Binding)

1: All Debts contracted and Engagements entered into, before the Adoption of this Constitution, shall be as valid against the United States under this Constitution, as under the Confederation.

2: This Constitution, and the Laws of the United States which shall be made in Pursuance thereof; and all Treaties made, or which shall be made, under the Authority of the United States, shall be the

supreme Law of the Land; and the Judges in every State shall be
bound thereby, any Thing in the Constitution or Laws of any State
to the Contrary notwithstanding.

3: The Senators and Representatives before mentioned, and the
Members of the several State Legislatures, and all executive and
judicial Officers, both of the United States and of the several
States, shall be bound by Oath or Affirmation, to support this
Constitution; but no religious Test shall ever be required as a
Qualification to any Office or public Trust under the United States.

> **Clauses 2 and 3 are no throwaways!** #2 declares the force of the
> contract. #3 demands that all constitutional officers promise to
> obey the constitution! And notice "...*the Judges in every State shall be
> bound thereby...*"
>
> This is quite the crux, isn't it? It is the law that regulates the
> regulators, polices the police and governs government. This is
> further clarified by Amendments 9 and 10.

Article VII (Ratification)

The Ratification of the Conventions of nine States, shall be
sufficient for the Establishment of this Constitution between the
States so ratifying the Same.

> Well, that's it for the constitution's main body. What follows are
> the amendments, which are just as much The Law as the preceding
> words.

The Amendments

Amendments to the US Constitution are appended to the unaltered original text. That provides an easily accessible touchstone to societal changes versus original intent. Many state constitutions, however, are amended by altering the text of the constitution. That makes it a historical research operation to determine original intent or original authority in these constitutions.

The first ten amendments to our federal constitution are called "The Bill of Rights." Many of the constitution's signers thought that a Bill of Rights was unnecessary; since they felt it obvious that federal government had only the powers specifically granted to it within the text of the US Constitution.

But perhaps our wisest founder, George Mason, refused to sign the Constitution without such a declaration of rights (thus ending his friendship with George Washington). But in 1791 (four years after the Constitutional Convention), the Bill of Rights was appended onto the Constitution.

Good thing, too, since what was considered a needless declaration of freedoms has become a tattered reminder of past liberties. In reading these you'll see very clearly just how far we've fallen.

We can't pick and choose which freedoms we want; you get them all as written, or we've got only conditional, and vanishing, privileges. In other words, we don't have any legal protection from politics when politicians feel free to violate these laws!

Amendment I (Authority Denied)

Congress shall make no law respecting an establishment of religion, or prohibiting the free exercise thereof; or abridging the freedom of speech, or of the press; or the right of the people peaceably to assemble, and to petition the Government for a redress of grievances.

"*Congress shall make no law respecting...*" is the operative phrase. Congress is banned from writing any laws about any of the freedoms listed, or "enumerated," in this amendment. Congress is the only federal lawmaking body, so there can be NO federal laws respecting these six freedoms. With such laws forbidden, there can be nothing for the executive branch to execute, and nothing for the federal judicial branch to judge.

This is a total gag order upon any federal authority in matters of religious institutions, religious practices, speech, press, peaceful assembly, and petitions to the federal government.

There are of course now thousands of thousands of "federal" laws, prohibitions, restrictions and provisos to each of these freedoms. And the freedom **of** religion has become freedom **from** religion; the opposite of what was intended and plainly written as law... And exactly the opposite of the interpretation the media gives to freedoms #3 and 4 in this amendment; even though the freedoms are separated by only the word, "*or*"!

Would the media allow any politician to treat reporters like Ten Commandment displays or Christmas trees; with "a veil of separation" between the government and the press? Maybe today.

Amendment II (Citizen Militia)

A well-regulated Militia, being necessary to the security of a free State, the right of the people to keep and bear Arms, shall not be infringed.

Here is the Virginia Constitution Bill of Rights, Section 13: "*That a well-regulated militia, composed of the body of the people, trained to arms, is the proper, natural, and safe defense of a free state, therefore, the right of the people to keep and bear arms shall not be infringed; that standing armies, in time of peace, should be avoided as dangerous to liberty; and that in all cases the military should be under strict subordination to, and governed by, the civil power.*"

The Tennessee Constitution's Article I, Section 24 is similar, though I like this phrase: *"That the sure and certain defense of a free people, is a well-regulated militia…"*

State militias, not federal armed forces, are supposed to be a republic's impenetrable defensive force. We were never to have a global military-industrial empire that benefits only a few, and bullies the world. We, as individual citizens, were supposed to take *personal* responsibility for our nation's violent force.

Doesn't it make sense that militia members would be much less likely to vote for warmongering politicians; particularly those with dual citizenship with other nations? Would militia members want to leave their jobs and families to go fight foreigners they know nothing about on foreign soil?

Today, most proponents of domestic disarmament, simultaneously support arming Israelis, Ukrainians and other foreign citizens with weapons forbidden here. We're global arms dealers, for Pete's sake! What hypocrisy!

And talk about internal contradiction… Democrats crying "defund the police," want a government that requires *more* police to enforce its authoritarian taxes, mandates and prohibitions. Republicans who cling to their rights to arms (without the militia part, by the way), claim they'll need their guns to fight the armed forces of government that they want to make more heavily-armed! And both parties have fallen head-over-heels for endless war.

The Posse Comitatus Act of 1878, which severely limited the use of federal military to enforce domestic policy, is nullified by erasing the distinction between military and domestic armed force. Mayor Giuliani bragged that his NYC police force was the fifth largest army in the world.

All the above is in direct opposition to this amendment.

The founders wrote exhaustively on this subject, and there is no room for equivocation. The founders wanted *citizens* to be at least as heavily armed, and trained in those arms, as the Swiss or Israeli

militias. The **states** would never limit citizens' right to protect
them against any force that could overwhelm the states. Most state
constitutions still strongly affirm this. Only five, California,
Maryland, Minnesota, New Jersey, and New York, do not.

There are two very significant aspects of citizen militias:
1. In recent history, even relatively leaderless, chaotic militias are
   practically impossible to subjugate.
2. Citizens expected to fight are much, much less-likely to agree to
   entangling foreign alliances and foreign wars.

Fundamental to a "well-regulated Militia" in both federal and state
constitutions is that **citizens take *personal* responsibility for
their nation's violence**; both in their choices on Election Day,
and when taking up arms against a fellow mortal human.

Most of us, including most 2A proponents who ignore the militia
phrase, can't fathom the militia-comprehensive view anymore,
though it's both proven correct, and literally ancient. That's a
shame, because we're ignoring all the lessons of human history and
human behavior since Cain slew Abel when we get this wrong.

Henry St. George Tucker, in his 1803 edition of *Blackstone's
Commentaries on the Laws of England*, wrote of this amendment, "*This
may be considered as the true palladium of liberty… The right of self defence is
the first law of nature: in most governments it has been the study of rulers to
confine this right within the narrowest limits possible. Wherever standing
armies are kept up, and the right of the people to keep and bear arms is, under
any colour or pretext whatsoever, prohibited, liberty, if not already annihilated,
is on the brink of destruction.*"

We live under a government that doesn't want citizens to protect
themselves from history's gallery of genocidal rogues.

Turn around a common phrase you've no doubt heard before…
"If politicians aren't doing anything wrong, then they have nothing
to fear …from armed citizens," right?

Consider the racist, oppressive origin of gun control laws, and the
number of times the 2nd Amendment served minorities. Look up

Amendment III (Military Occupation)

No Soldier shall, in time of peace be quartered in any house,
without the consent of the Owner, nor in time of war, but in a
manner to be prescribed by law.

This one's safe for now. A related issue of eminent domain is a
massive concern, but that's addressed in Amendment V. Standing
armies and increasingly militarized police, and a fierce fear/
aggression syndrome are much bigger problems.

Amendment IV (Security and Privacy)

The right of the people to be secure in their persons, houses,
papers, and effects, against unreasonable searches and seizures,
shall not be violated, and no Warrants shall issue, but upon
probable cause, supported by Oath or affirmation, and particularly
describing the place to be searched, and the persons or things to be
seized.

Amendments 4 and 5 have always been under attack. But during
the first Prohibition (between amendments 18 and 21), brutal
policing became accepted to the point that it now makes for
popular movies. We apparently like to watch perpetually stubble-
faced rogue cops break sissy rules as they break doors and skulls.

But the founders weren't worried about twisted cops so much as
renegade rulers. A thousand "make my day" cops can't cause the
trouble that a single Stalin or Hitler does.

Until recently, people had increasingly begged police to ignore
these amendments in order to catch pot smokers and pimps. But

now politicians are expanding civilian policing, and spying power to campus security guards, or to firemen, who aren't required to get search warrants before they enter a home. When will we get wise to what's at stake, and why we need to defend these laws?

Any people, *especially* government agents, who peek through our stuff, or take our stuff, or kick in doors and drag people out of their homes, or even snoop into their purchase or internet search history without having a properly authorized reason, are criminals. We should never think otherwise.

Amendment V (Liberty, Process and Property)

No person shall be held to answer for a capital, or otherwise infamous crime, unless on a presentment or indictment of a Grand Jury, except in cases arising in the land or naval forces, or in the Militia, when in actual service in time of War or public danger; nor shall any person be subject for the same offence to be twice put in jeopardy of life or limb; nor shall be compelled in any criminal case to be a witness against himself, nor be deprived of life, liberty, or property, without due process of law; nor shall private property be taken for public use, without just compensation.

Many have been forced to sell their property to mall developers and sports teams. And the "War on Drugs" lifted all inhibitions in this area. You could lose your car or other property if somebody **else** commits a drug offense in it! …*Without any compensation!*

Today, any of us can be called a "terrorist," and treated like one. Our income tax form has always been forced testimony that is used against us. But now, so is our library, texting, internet or purchase history; or, in fact...anything that can be detected by technology, or even surmised from probability algorithms.

Amendment VI (Prosecution Rights)

In all criminal prosecutions, the accused shall enjoy the right to a speedy and public trial, by an impartial jury of the State and district wherein the crime shall have been committed, which district shall have been previously ascertained by law, and to be informed of the nature and cause of the accusation; to be confronted with the witnesses against him; to have compulsory process for obtaining witnesses in his favor, and to have the Assistance of Counsel for his defence.

When does the term speedy ever apply? Impartial jury? …What do we think jury selection is all about? And long ago, judges started invoking the mystical incantation, "standing" to deny a person's day in court. And jury trials are very often denied as well.

But this unconstitutional injustice has stayed about the same for decades. Trial lawyers at least protect their profitable turf; and that's been a good thing for the most part. There are no *new* alarm bells specifically on the 6th. Not yet, anyway.

Amendment VII (Common Law)

In Suits at common law, where the value in controversy shall exceed twenty dollars, the right of trial by jury shall be preserved, and no fact tried by a jury, shall be otherwise re-examined in any Court of the United States, than according to the rules of the common law.

This amendment is mostly intact, aside from the now-paltry, but once significant $20, and our weakened trial by jury system.

But there's a lot of misunderstanding about civil, versus common or case law, just as there's misunderstanding about the jurisdictions of natural law, equity law, and maritime or admiralty law.

Case or common law is the body of prior judgments or legal precedents written by courts, as from English Law. Blackstone's *Commentaries on the Laws of England* are a methodical and even semi-constitutional set of writings. But even they are just a touchstone (and a huge one at that), as case law is an ever-changing thing, something like "the telephone game," or "whisper down the lane."

Civil law, from the Roman and even ancient Babylonian tradition, is law literally written, maybe even in stone, by legislators or kings. The constitution is a civil law compact that means exactly what it says. Judges have no power over it. Civil laws can be amended, discarded or replaced, but they're to be applied as written.

The source of law hierarchy is supposed to be first, constitutional; second, statutory; and third, case law. Constitutional and statutory law (state and federal code books) are written law.

The "Anti-Federalists" like Mason, Jefferson and Lee, knew about judges' tendency to acquire power over time by making everything into case law by precedent and ever-changing "interpretations."

But legislators also delegate power to appointed judges, who are unaccountable to voters, as a copout to their own electoral accountability. This thwarts a crucial check and balance.

Amendment VIII (Limited Punishment)

Excessive bail shall not be required, nor excessive fines imposed, nor cruel and unusual punishments inflicted.

Though the terms, "excessive" and "cruel and unusual" do leave wiggle room, the specifics of this amendment are still fairly healthy.

But far too many non-violent, victimless behaviors have been made illegal, and we therefore have too many people in jail. And half of them are there on "victimless crime" charges related to taxes and regulatory infractions.

We need to reconsider when and why it's necessary to ruin people's life forever by throwing them into a prison for statutory offenses.

Amendment IX (Enumerated Rights)

The enumeration in the Constitution, of certain rights, shall not be construed to deny or disparage others retained by the people.

Political leaders, wonks and activists often try to force-fit a non-speech behavior into the category of "free speech." What they're doing is denying the existence of this amendment, which gives people all the rights not specifically taken away by the constitution!

Flag burning isn't speech – it is flag burning; and we have the right to do it until that right is taken away by constitutional amendment. Smearing dung on an image of Virgin Mary may be offensive and stupid, but it's neither speech, nor prohibited, by any *federal* law.

On the other hand, we had full rights to our income until the 16th amendment arguably took that away. Politicians had no power to regulate the manufacture, distribution or sale of any product until the 18th amendment…a power that, by the way, they relinquished with the 21st amendment.

Amendments 9 and 10 provide an easy key to understanding the purpose and power of the US Constitution. These amendments nullify the "expansive" view of the "general welfare clause."

One simple question to determine whether a federal law, treaty or agency action is constitutional is, "What do citizens give up with this?" If we lose money, property or other rights not specifically taken away by amendment, then it's unconstitutional until or unless a proper constitutional amendment.

Amendment X (Federal Leash)

The powers not delegated to the United States by the Constitution, nor prohibited by it to the States, are reserved to the States respectively, or to the people.

This clarifies that our federal government has only the powers specifically granted to it by the US Constitution. Powers not specifically granted are hereby specifically denied! What people often call "vague" or "silent" is still, therefore, prohibited! *Most* of what our government does is therefore illegal!

"I consider the foundation of the Constitution as laid on this ground: That 'all powers not delegated to the United States, by the Constitution, nor prohibited by it to the States, are reserved to the States or to the people.' To take a single step beyond the boundaries thus specifically drawn around the powers of Congress is to take possession of a boundless field of power, no longer susceptible of any definition." –Thomas Jefferson, 1791.

In fact, we no longer have a **federal** government, since "federal" is defined as a limited, distributed government with sovereign states; more like the old EU than the current USA. We now have a **unitary**, or centralized almighty government.

What to do about it? Well, the clear intention of this amendment is to declare limits on federal power. Exceeding authority nullifies its legitimate power. Nullification is, in fact, the remedy to the breach of any of these constitutional delegations of power.

There were controversies in nullification, of course! Those who wanted to nullify something were strong proponents of nullification. But the same people, when they wanted power denied them by constitutions, became opponents of the whole idea. The famous anti-bankster firebrand, Andrew Jackson, opposed nullification when it ran against his interests, but favored it against the unconstitutional banking.

So there was something of a "nullification crisis" in 1828-33 that, unfortunately, didn't lead to much nullification. Instead, it provoked stewing resentments, and the War Between the States.

Anyway, the preceding was the Bill of Rights. A total of ten single sentences that affirm the rights of citizens over their government. We should know them all. We should insist upon them every day by whatever means we have; and of course we should defend them in the voting booth.

Amendment XI (Limited Jurisdiction)

The Judicial power of the United States shall not be construed to
extend to any suit in law or equity, commenced or prosecuted
against one of the United States by Citizens of another State, or by
Citizens or Subjects of any Foreign State.

As previously mentioned, this amendment more specifically limits
the power of courts. Unfortunately, this amendment has come to
mean that federal courts will not even hear a case when a state is
the defendant. In other words, a citizen can't sue his state in
federal court, unless the state consents to federal jurisdiction.

The author has butted his head against this one rather painfully.

Amendment XII (Electors)

The Electors shall meet in their respective states, and vote by ballot
for President and Vice-President, one of whom, at least, shall not
be an inhabitant of the same state with themselves; they shall name
in their ballots the person voted for as President, and in distinct
ballots the person voted for as Vice-President, and they shall make
distinct lists of all persons voted for as President, and of all persons
voted for as Vice-President, and of the number of votes for each,
which lists they shall sign and certify, and transmit sealed to the
seat of the government of the United States, directed to the
President of the Senate;--The President of the Senate shall, in the
presence of the Senate and House of Representatives, open all the
certificates and the votes shall then be counted;--The person
having the greatest number of votes for President, shall be the
President, if such number be a majority of the whole number of
Electors appointed; and if no person have such majority, then from
the persons having the highest numbers not exceeding three on the
list of those voted for as President, the House of Representatives
shall choose immediately, by ballot, the President. But in choosing
the President, the votes shall be taken by states, the representation

from each state having one vote; a quorum for this purpose shall consist of a member or members from two-thirds of the states, and a majority of all the states shall be necessary to a choice. And if the House of Representatives shall not choose a President whenever the right of choice shall devolve upon them, before the fourth day of March next following, then the Vice-President shall act as President, as in the case of the death or other constitutional disability of the President. --The person having the greatest number of votes as Vice-President, shall be the Vice-President, if such number be a majority of the whole number of Electors appointed, and if no person have a majority, then from the two highest numbers on the list, the Senate shall choose the Vice-President; a quorum for the purpose shall consist of two-thirds of the whole number of Senators, and a majority of the whole number shall be necessary to a choice. But no person constitutionally ineligible to the office of President shall be eligible to that of Vice-President of the United States.

We're told today that, in spite of what Hamilton wrote in Federalist no.68, that "…*the **people** of each State shall choose a number of persons as electors*," citizens never voted for the electoral college electors. That's not true; and we've only made "the people" abstracted into political party and legislature choices. But we'll discuss this more later. What's maybe equally impactful, is that before this amendment, the VP would be the candidate who came in second in the voting. That was probably a good idea, as it prevented too much partisan domination all at once…and made political infighting both invigorating and inherently limited the concentration of federal power.

Notice that all previous amendments were one-sentence apiece, and dealt more with authority than detail. The details and effect of this amendment could have been achieved by legislation; though in this case, what was achieved was dubious, at best. It was intended to prevent ties and deadlocks, but made our politics more malleable to the power of political parties. The amendment followed the partisan kerfuffle of 1796, and the hilariously fractious election of

1800, so it's understandable that politicians felt the nation's mood needed calming assurance that separate ballots would be cast for both POTUS and VPOTUS, and only one of each from each state. But this was the first really dumb amendment – made dumber by the fact that we let partisan POTUS candidates choose their running mates and no longer elect VPs as constitutionally described. And that allows a concentration of partisan power our founders warned us against.

And we don't even do this anymore, now that the parties combine the POTUS and VPOTUS into a single, one-party entity.

Amendment XIII (Slavery Prohibited)

Neither slavery nor involuntary servitude, except as a punishment for crime whereof the party shall have been duly convicted, shall exist within the United States, or any place subject to their jurisdiction.

Congress shall have power to enforce this article by appropriate legislation.

This amendment, of course prohibits slavery that was once allowed as a state jurisdictional issue. But it also has implications today, besides the fact that there are actually more slaves, mostly as sex slaves, in our country today than when this amendment was written. One theoretically could choose to avoid any work, and thus avoid the involuntary servitude inherent in income and payroll taxes. But then, others are involuntarily forced to support such a person's government assistance. In any case, XIII is violated by the fact that at least some percentage of our labor is mandatorily taken for the government. This argument, however, could apply to any form of taxation but user fees such as sales tax, and a form of property tax that isn't commonly used. And it's not reasonable to expect any government to run without any taxation at all.

But the sentence ("*Congress shall have power to enforce this article by appropriate legislation.*") introduces an error that is mindlessly repeated from this amendment through amendment XXVI.

Of course Congress can legislate what is authorized by this amendment. But only the Executive Branch has any enforcement powers. At best this sentence is unnecessary. More likely it confounds a clear understanding and application of separated powers among both citizens and politicians.

Amendment XIV (Reconstruction)

1: All persons born or naturalized in the United States, and subject to the jurisdiction thereof, are citizens of the United States and of the State wherein they reside. No State shall make or enforce any law which shall abridge the privileges or immunities of citizens of the United States; nor shall any State deprive any person of life, liberty, or property, without due process of law; nor deny to any person within its jurisdiction the equal protection of the laws.

This long, multi-issue amendment has often been confusingly, destructively "interpreted" from the start. Of divisive relevance as this book goes to print is the very first sentence; specifically, "*All persons born or naturalized in the United States, and subject to the jurisdiction thereof, are citizens of the United States…*"

This is where we get the concept and buzzword, "birthright citizenship."

The intention was to overturn the *Dred Scott* decision, and affirm that states couldn't deny citizen rights to newly freed slaves. But the wording was problematic. The "*…and subject to the jurisdiction thereof*" clause, for example, intentionally excluded Native Americans living under tribal sovereignty. Some freed slaves joined Native American tribes, so were not citizens of the USA. Children born of foreign diplomats have been another exception.

So…if a pregnant Mexican dives across the border and delivers a baby in the USA end zone, is it a citizenship touch-down, or not? Is she or the child subject to the jurisdiction of the USA, or not? Is she even an *illegal* alien if she's *not* subject to USA jurisdiction? Such are questions that courts have said need to be addressed by legislation.

However, the 1985 case *Rios-Pineda v. U.S. Dept. of Justice, I.N.S.* held that a child born in the USA of illegal aliens, was, in fact, a USA citizen. The concept of birthright citizenship (or being subject to the land's King) is ancient, and even canonized by Blackstone in English Law. On the other hand, Thomas Jefferson rebelled against citizenship by "chance and not choice." You decide. This amendment is badly worded.

The rest of this first section of the 14th has been less contentious, and fixed the prior issue that states could impose some oppressions on its inhabitants as long as:

1. All states did the same thing uniformly, and,
2. Such oppression didn't defy the limitations imposed on states by Article IV, Sect. 2.

In other words, a state could theoretically deny a state citizen rights to free speech, to bear arms, etc., as long as other states did so as well. Those rights (powers denied federal government and reserved for citizens…and states) were previously limits on only the federal government. That part is commonly, though dimly, understood, but a core principle of federalism.

What most conclude from this amendment is that the federal government herewith assumes sovereignty over the states in civil rights; the states becoming subunits of the greater central government. That's not true. It's (perhaps unintentionally) an affirmation that **citizens are constitutionally sovereign over every level of their government!**

This takes away the states' previously superior power, and makes federal citizen rights universal. In other words, states may no longer deny any citizen the enumerated rights to arms, religion, etc., or the expansive individual rights of the federal ninth amendment, and the restrictions imposed on politicians by the tenth.

And please note "...*equal protection of the laws.*" As previously discussed, using a set of state law examples, this phrase very concisely invalidates and nullifies most of what we call the "Two Party System," as previously detailed.

This amendment does *not* grant the federal government more power, as some anti-14A "patriots" claim – it guarantees citizens more rights by denying states' power to take them away!

About *Roe v Wade*:

This isn't the book to discuss the social, moral or personal issues inherent in abortion. What follows is only the constitutional issue. And in writing for the majority opinion in the 1973 decision, Justice Harry Blackmun was correct in one sense – the 14th Amendment does assert both 9th rights and 10th Amendment protections for all citizens in all states; including privacy. Our government certainly doesn't protect our privacy right today!

But ...is abortion a ***right*** of a mother, or a ***crime*** against a child? What sort of entity is a fetus? Isn't this the crux of our conflicts?

Natural rights aren't *granted* by the federal government – they're *protected* by prohibiting government – any level of government – from denying people those rights.

But we expect government to do something about crime.

Crimes and torts, or harm against actual victims, including murder, are state-only jurisdiction with the exception of the federal crimes listed in this constitution. So, if the child is any part of this, it's a state issue, not federal issue, and *Roe v Wade* was correctly nullified.

If this were about state laws, a much larger set of constitutional issues would arise, including fathers' rights and responsibilities with abortion versus child support. The federal issue is simpler, though still, obviously and passionately, controversial.

2: Representatives shall be apportioned among the several States according to their respective numbers, counting the whole number of persons in each State, excluding Indians not taxed. But when the right to vote at any election for the choice of electors for President and Vice President of the United States, Representatives in Congress, the Executive and Judicial officers of a State, or the members of the Legislature thereof, is denied to any of the male inhabitants of such State, being twenty-one years of age, and citizens of the United States, or in any way abridged, except for participation in rebellion, or other crime, the basis of representation therein shall be reduced in the proportion which the number of such male citizens shall bear to the whole number of male citizens twenty-one years of age in such State.

This part did a number of things, but don't ignore the part about electors. This is **very** important today: "*…the right to vote at any election for the choice of* **electors** *for President and Vice President of the United States…*" In addition to voting for other officials, we are STILL supposed to have the power to **vote for electors in the Electoral College!** And any state that denies that power is to be severely punished by reduced representation in the legislature!

Would that change how we view the Electoral College today?

The constitution's original authors were divided on whether electors were to be chosen by state legislators, or directly by the people, so some state legislators appointed electors, and even by the post-civil-war era, some states still agreed with Alexander Hamilton's assessment that, "*a small number of persons,* **selected by their fellow-citizens** *from the general mass, will be most likely to possess the information and discernment requisite to such complicated investigations.*"

But this part of the 14th A was pretty completely ignored by the late 1930's when states stopped even listing the Electors on ballots. There's never been a good case for what we do today, letting

3: No person shall be a Senator or Representative in Congress, or
elector of President and Vice President, or hold any office, civil or
military, under the United States, or under any State, who, having
previously taken an oath, as a member of Congress, or as an officer
of the United States, or as a member of any State legislature, or as
an executive or judicial officer of any State, to support the
Constitution of the United States, shall have engaged in
insurrection or rebellion against the same, or given aid or comfort
to the enemies thereof. But Congress may by a vote of two-thirds
of each House, remove such disability.

4: The validity of the public debt of the United States, authorized
by law, including debts incurred for payment of pensions and
bounties for services in suppressing insurrection or rebellion, shall
not be questioned. But neither the United States nor any State
shall assume or pay any debt or obligation incurred in aid of
insurrection or rebellion against the United States, or any claim for
the loss or emancipation of any slave; but all such debts,
obligations and claims shall be held illegal and void.

Don't ignore the phrase, "...*authorized by law*!" The rather
vindictive origin of this clause aside, Amendment 10 is *our* tool for
nullifying laws, agencies, actions, powers and ...yes...debts.

5: The Congress shall have power to enforce, by appropriate
legislation, the provisions of this article.

The rest of the preceding amendment was written in a very difficult
era. But it's a bad idea to make amendments more procedural and
temporal than about authority. And that clause 5 is now a habit.

Amendment XV (All Men May Vote)

The right of citizens of the United States to vote shall not be
denied or abridged by the United States or by any State on account
of race, color, or previous condition of servitude.

The Congress shall have power to enforce this article by
appropriate legislation.

This is a short amendment; well in the spirit of the forefathers'
design – excepting that they really meant only men at this point,
and this was already part of Amendment XIV. And that last
sentence is, as previously mentioned, needless and inappropriate.

The federal government had never prohibited anyone from voting.
That was a state-issue. What this amendment did, if it wasn't clear
enough from the previous amendment, is guarantee that states
couldn't withhold the right to vote from any citizen because of
race, including former slaves.

Amendment XVI (Income Tax)

The Congress shall have power to lay and collect taxes on incomes,
from whatever source derived, without apportionment among the
several States, and without regard to any census or enumeration.

Some argue that this amendment is null and void because it was
improperly ratified (there's some truth to this). Others say it's null
because "incomes" has been repeatedly defined as just about
anything **but** wages. But that's all irrelevant. Voters and taxpayers
have repeatedly affirmed these words as law. And these words are
an authorization of tax on incomes ...from any source. Both by
practice and by neglectful violations of the constitutions, what we
have is what we've chosen for ourselves.

We should nullify the IRS and the collection of income tax as they
exist today if for no reason other than that they violate and

Amendment XVII (Election of Senators)

1: The Senate of the United States shall be composed of two Senators from each State, elected by the people thereof, for six years; and each Senator shall have one vote. The electors in each State shall have the qualifications requisite for electors of the most numerous branch of the State legislatures.

2: When vacancies happen in the representation of any State in the Senate, the executive authority of such State shall issue writs of election to fill such vacancies: Provided, That the legislature of any State may empower the executive thereof to make temporary appointments until the people fill the vacancies by election as the legislature may direct.

3: This amendment shall not be so construed as to affect the election or term of any Senator chosen before it becomes valid as part of the Constitution.

Amendment XVIII (Prohibition)

1: After one year from the ratification of this article the manufacture, sale, or transportation of intoxicating liquors within, the importation thereof into, or the exportation thereof from the United States and all territory subject to the jurisdiction thereof for beverage purposes is hereby prohibited.

2: The Congress and the several States shall have concurrent power to enforce this article by appropriate legislation.

3: This article shall be inoperative unless it shall have been ratified as an amendment to the Constitution by the legislatures of the several States, as provided in the Constitution, within seven years from the date of the submission hereof to the States by the Congress.

This was one of four amendments from the "Progressive Movement," including the 16th, 17th and 19th Amendments.

So much could be said here, but here are two key points:

1. This amendment properly, albeit with grammatical criminality, granted the federal government authority to ban ***only*** the *"manufacture, sale, or transportation of intoxicating liquors"* within the states, territories, and all federal plenary jurisdiction. It did **NOT** grant any authority to ban the **consumption** of intoxicating liquors...or anything else. The federal government has never been granted that natural law jurisdictional authority.

2. This limited authority was **repealed** by the 21st Amendment, and replaced by...nothing!

Somehow, however, this amendment was interpreted to mean the purchase and consumption of liquor was also banned. Over-aggressive enforcement of that interpretation by a habitually rogue agency now called the ATF killed more than 10,000 people by the intentional poisoning of alcohol supplies.

Happily, there is no longer any constitutional federal authority to ban the manufacture, sale, or transportation of *anything*. And there never was any federal authority to ban the purchase or consumption of *anything*. Sadly, our government has nevertheless taken this power without authority, and without limits.

Amendment XIX (Women Are Citizens Too)

The right of citizens of the United States to vote shall not be denied or abridged by the United States or by any State on account of sex.

Congress shall have power to enforce this article by appropriate legislation.

Once again, the second sentence is wrong. But otherwise, this is short and simple. But note that it's still only citizens who have the specific right to vote. Now that some states have allowed non-citizens the power to vote (only local elections so far), we have more issues brewing…

Amendment XX (Bunch of Details)

1: The terms of the President and Vice President shall end at noon on the 20th day of January, and the terms of Senators and Representatives at noon on the 3d day of January, of the years in which such terms would have ended if this article had not been ratified; and the terms of their successors shall then begin.

2: The Congress shall assemble at least once in every year, and such meeting shall begin at noon on the 3d day of January, unless they shall by law appoint a different day.

3: If, at the time fixed for the beginning of the term of the President, the President elect shall have died, the Vice President elect shall become President. If a President shall not have been chosen before the time fixed for the beginning of his term, or if the President elect shall have failed to qualify, then the Vice President elect shall act as President until a President shall have qualified; and the Congress may by law provide for the case wherein neither a President elect nor a Vice President elect shall have qualified, declaring who shall then act as President, or the manner in which one who is to act shall be selected, and such person shall act accordingly until a President or Vice President shall have qualified.

4: The Congress may by law provide for the case of the death of any of the persons from whom the House of Representatives may choose a President whenever the right of choice shall have devolved upon them, and for the case of the death of any of the persons from whom the Senate may choose a Vice President whenever the right of choice shall have devolved upon them.

5: Sections 1 and 2 shall take effect on the 15th day of October following the ratification of this article.

6: This article shall be inoperative unless it shall have been ratified as an amendment to the Constitution by the legislatures of three-fourths of the several States within seven years from the date of its submission.

Amendment XXI (Power to Prohibit Repealed)

1: The eighteenth article of amendment to the Constitution of the United States is hereby repealed.

2: The transportation or importation into any State, Territory, or possession of the United States for delivery or use therein of intoxicating liquors, in violation of the laws thereof, is hereby prohibited.

3: This article shall be inoperative unless it shall have been ratified as an amendment to the Constitution by conventions in the several States, as provided in the Constitution, within seven years from the date of the submission hereof to the States by the Congress.

> OK, fine. The 18th Amendment was dumb. Good riddance. It's a shame we've not similarly repealed the 16th and 17th Amendments. But there's a problem in clause 2. The statement, *"in violation of the laws thereof, is hereby prohibited"* contradicts the superior rights granted by the 14th Amendment, or at least raises questions of jurisdictional limits and constitutional integrity, unless any states had amended their constitutions to prohibit booze transportation under their own corporate, or admiralty/maritime jurisdiction. And none had.

Amendment XXII (Presidential Term Limits)

1: No person shall be elected to the office of the President more than twice, and no person who has held the office of President, or acted as President, for more than two years of a term to which some other person was elected President shall be elected to the office of the President more than once. But this article shall not apply to any person holding the office of President when this article was proposed by the Congress, and shall not prevent any person who may be holding the office of President, or acting as President, during the term within which this article becomes operative from holding the office of President or acting as

President during the remainder of such term.

2: This article shall be inoperative unless it shall have been ratified as an amendment to the Constitution by the legislatures of three-fourths of the several states within seven years from the date of its submission to the states by the Congress.

> In principle, term limits are what voters are supposed to do. But most voters want term limits to apply to all federal officers. Today we should put term limits on the heads of executive agencies and partisan staffers, too. But again, this is mostly details when it should've been about authority to write legislation by federal code. And that clause 2 is another embarrassingly needless repetition.

Amendment XXIII (D.C. Gets Representation in D.C.)

1: The District constituting the seat of government of the United States shall appoint in such manner as the Congress may direct: A number of electors of President and Vice President equal to the whole number of Senators and Representatives in Congress to which the District would be entitled if it were a state, but in no event more than the least populous state; they shall be in addition to those appointed by the states, but they shall be considered, for the purposes of the election of President and Vice President, to be electors appointed by a state; and they shall meet in the District and perform such duties as provided by the twelfth article of amendment.

2: The Congress shall have power to enforce this article by appropriate legislation.

> Congress already had plenary power over the district, and could've accomplished this by legislation without amendment. But this is also ignoring the reason the district was supposed to be the district,

the seat of federal power, and ***not*** *a state.* You can today see, by the wealth of the district and the extraordinary power therein contained, that giving it the power of a state is a stupidly dangerous corruption.

I'll not mention that last sentence anymore.

Amendment XXIV (Poll Tax)

1. The right of citizens of the United States to vote in any primary or other election for President or Vice President, for electors for President or Vice President, or for Senator or Representative in Congress, shall not be denied or abridged by the United States or any state by reason of failure to pay any poll tax or other tax.

Again… ***We The People are supposed to vote for the Electors of the Electoral College!*** Notice, too, that this 1964 Amendment is the first mention of Primary Elections, which were becoming widespread at about that time – a partisan travesty.

This doesn't prohibit poll taxes! It says only that we can vote even if we don't pay it. Perhaps it was worded like this because it was 1964 and politicians/culture had already devolved to a sad state of ignorant confusion.

2. The Congress shall have power to enforce this article by appropriate legislation.

Amendment XXV (Presidential Succession)

1: In case of the removal of the President from office or of his death or resignation, the Vice President shall become President.

2: Whenever there is a vacancy in the office of the Vice President, the President shall nominate a Vice President who shall take office upon confirmation by a majority vote of both Houses of Congress.

3: Whenever the President transmits to the President pro tempore of the Senate and the Speaker of the House of Representatives his written declaration that he is unable to discharge the powers and duties of his office, and until he transmits to them a written declaration to the contrary, such powers and duties shall be discharged by the Vice President as Acting President.

4: Whenever the Vice President and a majority of either the principal officers of the executive departments or of such other body as Congress may by law provide, transmit to the President pro tempore of the Senate and the Speaker of the House of Representatives their written declaration that the President is unable to discharge the powers and duties of his office, the Vice President shall immediately assume the powers and duties of the office as Acting President.

Thereafter, when the President transmits to the President pro tempore of the Senate and the Speaker of the House of Representatives his written declaration that no inability exists, he shall resume the powers and duties of his office unless the Vice President and a majority of either the principal officers of the executive department or of such other body as Congress may by law provide, transmit within four days to the President pro tempore of the Senate and the Speaker of the House of Representatives their written declaration that the President is unable to discharge the powers and duties of his office. Thereupon Congress shall decide the issue, assembling within forty-eight hours for that purpose if not in session. If the Congress, within twenty-one days after receipt of the latter written declaration, or, if Congress is not in session, within twenty-one days after Congress is required to assemble, determines by two-thirds vote of both Houses that the President is unable to discharge the powers and duties of his office, the Vice President shall continue to discharge the same as Acting President; otherwise, the President shall resume the powers and duties of his office.

Amendment XXVI (Teen Vote)

1: The right of citizens of the United States, who are 18 years of age or older, to vote, shall not be denied or abridged by the United States or any state on account of age.

2: The Congress shall have the power to enforce this article by appropriate legislation.

Amendment XXVII (Congressional Pay)

No law varying the compensation for the services of the Senators and Representatives shall take effect until an election of Representatives shall have intervened.

So, how *can* we *fix* this?

"ARTICLE I. Declaration of Rights.

Section 1. That all power is inherent in the people, and all free governments are founded on their authority, and instituted for their peace, safety, and happiness; for the advancement of those ends they have at all times, an unalienable and indefeasible right to alter, reform, or abolish the government in such manner as they may think proper.

Section 2. That government being instituted for the common benefit, the doctrine of nonresistance against arbitrary power and oppression is absurd, slavish, and destructive of the good and happiness of mankind." – Tennessee state constitution; very similar to the New Hampshire Constitution's *"Right of Revolution"*!!

First of all, what do we want? What are we willing to do to get it? If we had it, would we sustain it?? Is there some compromise that would satisfy us enough that we'd quit fighting each other and simply live, in peace, prosperity, security and freedom …and be happy?

It's all our choice. All us. We have all the power! What follows are the author's recommendations, obviously. But the choice is inherently collective. Talk to your friends and neighbors. Maybe try to find some common ground with enemies. We've got to collectively make this work.

Please note: It is not an oversight to omit the popular "Article V Convention," "Convention of States" or COS initiatives from the following suggestions. The method of proposing amendments is correct, but too many COS proponents are putting blind faith in the politicians already violating our state and federal constitutions, to change our constitution!

This is a dangerous self-deception and copout. Our federal constitution, with even the worst existing amendments, is far better than what we're doing. And so far, all of the proposals made by COS proponents aim to fix violations of the constitution by…changing the constitution? Bad logic.

It is also not an oversight that this book never fully addresses the "Two Nations," or United States, Inc., versus United States of America corruption involving land titles, common law, natural law and equity law. It is true that between our nation's 1787's debts, 1871's banker's demands, and FDR's New Deal, there were significant shenanigans. But it's also by our collective choices, past and present, that the problems exist, and persist.

In a different way, and as much as alternative voting schemes like Condorcet and Approval voting have strong advantages, none can fix voters' bad choices. Alternative voting schemes could reduce the dominance of our Two-Party puppet show, and open elections to real competition. And voting methods are in the state domain — much easier to pass than federal law. So such schemes, especially if combined with the elimination of Primary Elections, would almost surely be an improvement, and safer than a COS in the hands of our incumbent Powers That Be. But the arguments made against such schemes are mostly that, even with alternative parties already on the ballot, over 90% of us *still* vote for only the two dominant parties, no matter what. We must *still* fix *ourselves, first.*

Similarly, term limits are both popular, and good. Several bills have been proposed, and keep getting swept under the congressional rug. Why? Because our words say we want term limits, but our votes say we love incumbents and want them to stay in office until they die of mildew.

We cannot delegate our mess away. We cannot wait for others to perform magic. It is all on *us*, because our government *is* us. It is better to beat this point to death than to have our government beat us to death:

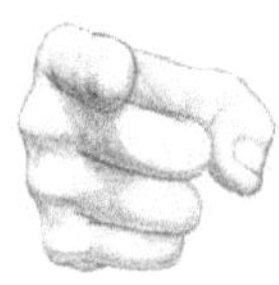

> All improvement has the same dependency – that we **FIRST** *change our choices!* - **Our** choices. **Us.** There is no magical procedure to fix what we've chosen for ourselves. All revolutions start in the heart, and mind.

The common saying, *"if voting changed anything, they'd make it illegal"* is misattributed to everyone from Emma Goldman, to Mark Twain and Albert Einstein. But the saying is a copout. We're not even *trying* to vote for anything *different!* We instead tend to come up with games and excuses for sustaining the status quo's accelerating dash to the cliff of self-destruction. …And it *is* self-destruction by both cop-out, and delegation to people we claim to mistrust, yet keep re-electing. Probably misattributed to Sun Tzu, but observably true: *"An evil man will burn his own nation to the ground to rule over the ashes."* And we've a lot of evil men in high places these days.

Yet from asking scores of thousands of citizens how they vote:

1. We really do have what we've chosen. Most of us choose, pay for and submit to, what we say we don't want. And most of us *say* we have no choice but to do so.
2. Most don't really know what they're voting for. Most of even those who do some homework on candidates, fail to see the puppet strings and what's happening behind the curtains. Hopefully this book can help with this one…at least a little bit.
3. Many say there's a line that cannot be crossed; and when that line is crossed, they'll fight! But…
   A. The line keeps moving back, and back, and back, and…
   B. They surely won't fight for what they won't even vote for.

So, the first recommendation?

STOP voting for the Two-Party System!

The system is much bigger and wider than the parties and candidates themselves. And it's unfixable. Irredeemably corrupt. Furthermore, it does not want to be fixed. While those pulling the strings are fools failing to see how it will turn out for their own heirs, the ruling class likes things just the way they are. This is not to say you shouldn't vote for any Democrat or Republican (though that would be the fastest, safest, surest way to shake out the whole network). But we really, really must stop thinking that those parties are anything but a corrupt puppet show. It's rare that we ever get a Ron Paul, Justin Amash or Thomas Massie out of that giant partisan pustule infected with professional "bundlers," "political advisors" wonks, managers, and of course, corporations and even one particular foreign government, pulling the strings.

It's a shame that so many of the concepts and political lessons in the Bible are dismissed as mere religion. God's reply when the Israelites asked for a human king in I Samuel 8 is so relevant to our time that it echoes in every news item. The secular truth is that the litany of woe we create when we make false gods of political parties, or idols of political leaders never ends.

Mahatma Gandhi never actually said, *"Be the change you wish to see in the world."* But it's a great idea. Nothing gets better until we do.

So the second proposal may sound like, "Eat your broccoli," but it's the heart of any positive change in our society:

Live the Golden Rule

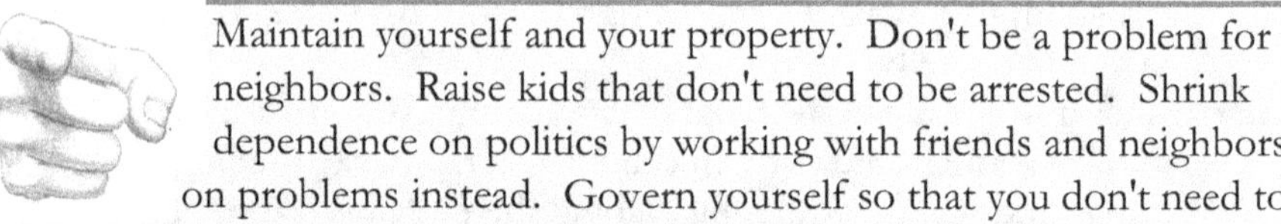

Maintain yourself and your property. Don't be a problem for neighbors. Raise kids that don't need to be arrested. Shrink dependence on politics by working with friends and neighbors on problems instead. Govern yourself so that you don't need to be governed. Work with your neighbors so that they don't need to be governed either. Be an *informed* and *accountable* voter. We really must **face our political reality!**

Our barbaric default authoritarianism is what we get when we fail to set and *maintain* a course for something better. This is like oral hygiene. We can't brush just once and be done with it. Crud keeps building up, and we must keep brushing it off. And if, like with today's politics, we let things go to the point of insanity, we need more than a simple brushing. We need to hit the flush lever. So a crucial and immediate recommendation is:

Make Better Choices - Now

No more holding our nose to re-elect "lesser evil." No more "baby steps" incrementalism that takes us backwards even faster. Let's make the next Election Day the peaceful revolution we need.

All the choice, *all* the power, and *all* the accountability, is **ours**. It's not so hard to run for public office, actually. It can be fun. It should be a noble service. But we can also look for, encourage and financially support better candidates. Would we really hire anybody for any other profession or even day labor the way we hire politicians? We should demand, attend, and participate in public forums and debates. We should not let candidates control our process. Expensive yard signs, billboards and campaign media shouldn't work on us. We shouldn't expect candidates to dive through advertisements to get our attention. We should make them fear our questions, and earn our votes. Edward Abbey wrote, "*Freedom …begins between the ears.*" Each generation must be informed, and make vastly better choices than we've been making. None of the following suggestions can work until we make better choices that lead to better politicians and better government.

And to that point:

End The Secrets

We have for too long tolerated secrecy sold to us as necessary to "National Security." That tolerance must end.

We The People have the power to choose our way of life simply by ticking boxes and punching buttons. Our choices should be based on true and complete information. It should be obvious to all that we're inundated by lies. But what's worse is what's missing from our information about everything important. With lies you can consider the source, listen to others, and decide for yourself. But what of the information we're denied?

1. By what's already declassified, or more often, leaked over the years, we know that very significant omissions from public discourse, such as the true reasons for war, causes of political deaths, political tricks and actions of our spy agencies, would have almost surely changed the course of elections, and today's culture, if only we'd had the facts.
2. If we can be trusted with voting, we need to be entrusted with the information upon which we're to vote. That means we need to vote for people who speak, and reveal, truth. All of it. ***End the secrecy.***
3. More importantly, we must consider that as knowledge is power, concentrated control of knowledge is very corrupting and dangerous. It's no secret that since their beginnings, the FBI and CIA have been corrupt, and have done horrible things …including blackmailing and manipulating our elected politicians. We'll always have spies. But they must be transparent and accountable to *all three* branches of our government. And there are far too many unaccountable leaders of our executive agency bureaucracy that need to be removed, and their agencies decimated.

Of course some of the secrecy is from both the immense size, cost, and unregulated condition of our government. So the next suggestion:

Constitutional Restoration/ Sunset Resolutions

No human, and not likely AI any time soon, could know all our laws or how to make them work. They're not only too numerous, but also self-contradictory, foolishly complex, counter-productive, and impossible to justly enforce. So we should refine and reduce the number of laws, and keep them few, simple and important so that our rules are:

- Few enough for everyone to know.
- Simple enough for everyone to understand.
- Important enough to enforce without exceptions or special classes.

Ideally, these resolutions would be followed by both state and federal constitutional amendments. All laws, rules, agencies, departments…every bit of government that is not already clearly inscribed in constitutions would be reviewed every ten years with a two-thirds majority vote to restore it by rewriting it, or let it die. Call it spring cleaning, constructive destruction, or whatever you like. We need to clean house in every respect.

> Introducing these sample resolutions for federal and state governments would at least open a discussion on what sort of nation we're to be; a nation or state with governed government, or a crime syndicate. Short and relatively simple, but they do strike at the root. And, importantly, by the votes on the resolutions you could see who among your representatives is a constitutional public servant, and who needs to go:

Federal resolution:

Whereas the plain wording of the 10th Amendment to the Constitution for the United States of America is binding law;

Be it resolved that;

No federal law, agency, program or international treaty that depends upon authority not specifically granted by the Constitution for the United States of America shall be valid;

Any federal agency, law, program or international treaty transcending authority specifically granted by the Constitution for the United States of America is null and void;

Unconstitutional laws, agencies, programs and treaties have created both problems and dependencies that will take time to rectify;

Therefore;

All unconstitutional federal powers, delegations, laws, programs, treaties and entities that cannot be immediately nullified must be phased out within no more than ten years.

State resolution (Indiana as example):
Whereas, the plain wording of Article I Section 25 of the Indiana Constitution, and Indiana Code 1-1-2: Sec. 1, and the 10th Amendment to the Constitution for the United States of America, is binding law;

Be it resolved that;

No state or federal law, agency, program or international treaty that depends upon authority not specifically granted by the Constitution of the State of Indiana, or Constitution for the United States of America, shall be valid;

Any state or federal agency, law, program or international treaty transcending authority specifically granted by the Constitution of the State of Indiana, or the Constitution for the United States of America is null and void;

Unconstitutional laws, agencies, programs and treaties have created both problems and dependencies that will take time to rectify;

Therefore;

All unconstitutional governing powers, delegations, laws, programs, treaties and entities that cannot be immediately nullified must be phased out within no more than ten years.

It is for good reasons that it is difficult to amend the constitution. It is in fact dangerous to initiate the amendment process given the people and parties we've empowered to carry out such amendments[48]. But the assumption in all these proposals is that We The People, in a glorious mass-epiphany, fire all the louts and bums, and we choose people of better ideology, caliber and civil morality. So, should this miracle occur, here're three ideas that would be helpful in clarifying what should be obvious from our founders' intentions and words:

Repeal the Amendments XVI and XVII

1. It has been proposed that if we were to eliminate the unconstitutional Federal Reserve System, we could eliminate income tax and replace it with nothing at no cost. That's not exactly true. But income tax, at least as implemented, is horrifically costly even on its own, in administrative, judicial and compliance costs, and a terrible tax all around. There are much better ways to raise revenue, but the assumption with this whole section is that we'll vote better, and thus reduce the need for so much revenue. So kill the 16th Amendment.
2. We need our truly bicameral congress back. States need a voice in Congress. So, kill the 17th Amendment.

Simplification and Sunset Amendment

1. Simplicity, timeliness and relevance being crucial to law and governance, no laws in the United States Code, and no federal agencies or offices not specifically authorized and delimited by the Constitution for the United States of America, shall exist for more ten years.
2. Laws, agencies and offices at ten years deemed both constitutional and beneficial, shall be reinstated only by new legislation passed by a two-thirds majority.
3. No legislation shall be passed that consists of more than 6000 words.

---

[48] The concern with the COS (Convention of States)/Article V proponents is that they too vaguely expect benefit from the people and parties that created and sustain the problems we need to fix. And most don't realize that the constitutions already contain what we want…if only we'd use them. A COS with our current electorate and power structure would more likely empower bad people to destroy what little remains of our constitutional rule of law.

Immediate Nullification Amendment

1. Any judicial, executive, legislative or bureaucratic ruling, law, agency or action, and any treaty, depending upon authority not specifically granted by this constitution, shall be null and void.
2. No law shall be passed, no agency shall be created and no action shall be taken that depends upon authority not specifically granted by this constitution.

Next, a couple of resolutions to clean-up our democratic processes and laws. These are inherently, by design, a state, not federal, domain. What follows is specific to Indiana, but it'd take only little work to craft similar resolutions for your own state:

Resolution to Restore Election Choices

HOUSE CONCURRENT RESOLUTION No. __

Whereas, the original constitutional design was so obviously for citizens to directly choose "Electoral College" electors for USA President, that Alexander Hamilton's proposed constitutional amendment (29 January 1802) to codify popular election of electors by district, was deemed unnecessary,

Whereas, Amendment XIV, Section 2 of the Constitution for the United States of America specifies severe penalties for states which deny citizens direct selection of electors,

Whereas, the original constitutional assumption was that citizens could "write-in" any person desired for any public office, and that there is no need or constitutional authority to limit citizens' choices of candidates,

Whereas, the states did not limit candidate choices for nearly 100 years, and then only gradually began limiting them such that now only ten states have no limits on voter choices, and 8 states completely forbid "write-in" votes,

Whereas, the first "primary elections" in the USA were "white primaries" in southern states after the Civil War,

Whereas, the more recent "closed primaries" have the intended effect of weakening alternative parties, entrenching power in only two factions, extending fundraising, thus promoting corruption, and limiting choices for the General Election,

Be it resolved by the House of Representatives of the General Assembly of the State of Indiana, the Senate concurring:

That the Indiana General Assembly resolves to establish, by appropriate legislation, election choice to all citizens, for all candidates and for all offices, including electors for the office of President and Vice President, of the United States of America.

Resolution to Restore Fair and Equal Ballot Access

HOUSE CONCURRENT RESOLUTION No. __

Whereas, Article I, Section 23 of the Indiana Constitution specifies that *"The General Assembly shall not grant to any citizen, or class of citizens, privileges or immunities, which, upon the same terms, shall not equally belong to all citizens,"*

Whereas, Article I, Section 25 clarifies that *"No law shall be passed, the taking effect of which shall be made to depend upon any authority, except as provided in this Constitution,"*

Whereas, Indiana Code properly subsumes itself under both state and federal constitutions in IC § 1-1-2-1;

Whereas, Indiana Code § 3 has over time, created special classes of citizens, with a hierarchy of ballot access and political affiliation rules, varying privileges, limitations or immunities, which, upon the same terms, do not equally belong to all citizens;

Whereas, examples of special class of citizens, privileges or immunities, which, upon the same terms, shall not equally belong to all citizens are found in IC § 3-5-1-2, IC § 3-5-2-5.5, IC § 3-5-2-30, IC § 3-5-3-7, IC § 3-6-4.1-2, IC § 3-10-1-2;

Whereas, these special classes of citizen with hierarchical rights, privileges, limitations and immunities present under Indiana Code § 3 violate both state and federal constitutional rule of law, as well as fundamental principles of fairness and equality under law;

Whereas, our founders forcefully warned against political parties, divisive factions, and specifically against a dominance of only two parties,

Be it resolved by the House of Representatives of the General Assembly of the State of Indiana, the Senate concurring:

SECTION 1. That the Indiana General Assembly recognizes both the errors made, and damages caused, by past legislation that promoted division and concentration of power into only two opposing factions.

SECTION 2. That the Indiana General Assembly resolves to remedy violations of individual rights and transgressions of constitutional rule of law present under Indiana Code § 3 by appropriate legislation, to allow fair and same campaign, ballot, party and election rules for all Hoosiers, regardless of partisan affiliation, or lack thereof.

LEASH OUR CORPORATIONS!

This one is absolutely critical, but so multi-pronged now that the specifics could become a whole other book. Mostly, voters must do a much better job of picking candidates. It's not hard to see a candidate's puppet strings in FEC filings as they exist today. But here are a few legislative suggestions toward the goal of making our government much less-fascist, and much more of a republic with fair elections and transparency:

1. END CORPORATE PERSONHOOD! This is absolutely essential. Immortal abstractions must ***not*** have human rights. And the principle that applies to governments of greater power needing greater accountability…and scrutiny, fits here.
2. Concomitant to the above, the 2010 SCOTUS ruling in *Citizens United v. Federal Election Commission* must be struck down. Unions, banks and other big corporations too often "speak" in ways that harm even the humans within the corporation itself. Not all teachers are OK with teacher unions' politics, and not all employees of Palantir are minions of Satan, for example. It's madness to allow each corporation a single voice in

politics, magnified by the combined resources of the
corporation.

3. End special exemptions from accountability such as the
    National Childhood Vaccine Injury Act of 1986, that removes
    vaccine manufacturers' liability for their products, and places
    burdens for injuries on taxpayers instead.

4. Corporations and corporate laws, with very few exceptions,
    should be state-level, not federal. International corporations
    aren't all evil. But their exceptional powers, granted by
    multiple governments, deserve exceptional scrutiny and
    restraint.

The next four proposals are the author's favorite, most fundamental
proposals promoted by DownsizeDC. But there are several other excellent
proposals at: https://archive.downsizedc.org/proposals/

One Subject at a Time

OSTA – One Subject at a Time Act (currently H.R.872 and S.110), *"requires
each bill or joint resolution to include no more than one subject and the subject to be
clearly and descriptively expressed in the measure's title. An appropriations bill may not
contain any general legislation or change to existing law that is not germane to the subject
of such bill. The bill voids measures or provisions noncompliant with these requirements,
including appropriation provisions outside the relevant subcommittee's jurisdiction."*

This would, if made law, and especially in combination with an enlarged
congress, make it much harder to pile unrelated rules, funding, corruption
and waste into huge, unreadable monstrosities of legislation. Read the
current text at https://archive.downsizedc.org/osta-text/.

Read the Bills

RTBA – Read the Bills Act, (currently S.103), has two key functions. First,
*"…the bill requires any measure introduced in either chamber to contain a provision
citing the specific powers granted to Congress in the Constitution to enact the proposed*

measure, including all of its provisions." But the bill must also meet specific publication/notice requirements, and be read, verbatim and in full, to the respective chamber.

This means that the bill must demonstrate that it's actually authorized by the constitution (what a refreshing change!), and that every member reads/hears every word of it before voting it into law. This, along with the above OSTA, would also discourage the multi-thousand-page bills we suffer today. Read the text of the current bill at https://archive.downsizedc.org/rtba-text/.

Write the Laws

WTLA – Write the Laws Act, (not yet introduced), is another proposal that DownsizeDC knocked out of the park, and really should be made law even before the previous proposals. It would address what was previously mentioned as our "Bureaucratic State" in the chapter, "How laws are supposed to work." This act would fix a major breach of constitutional design as well as the clear intent of our constitution's Article I, Section I. Read the proposed text at https://archive.downsizedc.org/the-official-text-of-downsize-dcs-write-the-laws-act-wtla/.

Free Competition in Currency

Ron Paul first introduced HR77, the Free Competition in Currency Act of 2013, to repeal the Coinage Act of 1965, which unconstitutionally decrees that, "*Federal Reserve notes and circulating notes of Federal Reserve banks and national banks, are legal tender for all debts, public charges, taxes, and dues,*" and allows for reestablishment of sound monetary policy, including free-market trade options such as cryptocurrency and privately-issued gold/silver coins.

We must End the Fed, return the accountability, and constitutionality, of federally-issued currency to Congress, and let the free market be free to trade with whatever works.

How do we actually repeal all this monetary mayhem, though, when so many powerful, secretive, and unquestionably evil people would be willing to do anything to protect their scam?

1. Repeal all "Legal Tender" laws. Allow free-market money, to replace corrupt monopoly paper. Let people do what they want with fiat paper, but also allow whatever alternatives they wish (gold coins, crypto, car parts, whatever). Government's only role would be in enforcement of contracts.

2. Freeze the # of fiat dollars as we phase them out of circulation.

3. Define the dollar on specie weight...preferably coin silver or gold.

4. Establish gold as a monetary reserve at the market ratio to silver.

5. Restore specie coinage at the mint. Coins' value according with metals and weights used.

6. Pay off the national debt with federal reserve notes.

7. Pledge the government's gold and silver to back Fed notes in circulation.

8. Determine the weight of all gold/silver held by the gov't, and rationalize it to the total number of fed notes in circulation.

9. Retire all Fed notes - redeem in specie.

10. Convert all contracts to real, specie-backed dollars.

11. Issue 100% backed silver certificates as the only paper money.

12. Abolish the Fed.

13. Deregulate banking and **end *their* protection**. No FDIC. If a bank fails, it fails, and others learn the lessons. Tough love, but there's no other way to protect the rest of us from transgenerational theft and corruption.

15. Reduce the size and scope of government as previously detailed by nullification and sunset provisions. Protection of life, liberty and property only. Sell all assets that don't apply to its sole mission.

16. Restore national independence/ sovereignty. Get out of the International Bank of Settlements, World Bank, etc.

Enlarge the House of Representatives

Given everything in this book so far, it may seem perverse to suggest *adding* politicians. But with the problems with over-large rural districts, the power of incumbency and money, isolating politicians from their constituents, and thus inevitable corruption, it starts to make sense why our nation's founders intended that we'd have proportionally many, many more US House Representatives than were fixed in *1929*…based on the *1910 census!*

James Madison wrote that districts with too few representatives would lack *"…the confidence of the people, and would be too sparsely taken from the people, to bring with them all the local information which would be frequently wanted."* He proposed a constitutional amendment that would have capped the population of each district to 50,000 citizens. Putting that in today's perspective, that would mean instead of 435 House reps as locked in by The Permanent Apportionment Act of 1929, there would be, today … …***66,000!***

- We have the technology to do this. The author has worked remote since the early 1990's, and many do so today. Consider how much different our access to federal politics would be if our representative was almost always in our district, and geographically much, much closer. Our reps don't need to fall asleep texting in the same big room.
- A lot of our reps don't even show up to work even half the time, and there are only from around 160 to 190 days when they're expected to show up anyway[49]. The incumbent in one of my own US House campaigns had been present only 1 day in 5 through the prior two-year term. Being closer to constituents, with less invisibility to playing hooky (or being near death, as is the case with many of our aging incumbents), would promote more accountability in general.
- Pork projects and sleazy behavior would be harder to sneak past more reps that don't hang out at the same clubs and golf courses.
- Half of K-Street is populated by special interest groups interested only in tax policy…or war, for example. Most of Washington D.C. is a

---

[49] OK, to be fair, I wish a lot of our congress critters would never show up.

theme park for corruption and political puppet masters. We really want to get our representatives out of that town, and safer from corruption.

- More representatives would make both the House, and the Electoral College, more representative of our population in geography, demographics and ideology.
- It's relatively cheap for large special interests to buy out a majority among only 535 reps. Even the military-industrial and financial complexes would have a much harder time purchasing even a thousand reps who lived and worked closer to their constituents.
- We'd be much more likely to know something about the people we hire for the job if they were more accessible to us before, and, crucially, *after*, Election Day.
- We've already got many, many more people in D.C.'s halls of power than just Senators and House Reps. There are currently ~10,700 congressional staffers alone. But they serve politicians, not us. And we need to get better at discerning who our politicians serve.

Sixty-six thousand reps aren't necessary, of course. Even a tenth, or twentieth of that number would be a massive, even revolutionary shift of power away from D.C., and back to us.

Of course, an argument against this proposal is that some deliberations and votes need to be secret, and/or highly secure.

But:
- Most things that require such security are already limited to only a relative few. Even expanding by that same percentage would require no change to travel or accommodation from present.
- If we can't secure communications among our federal officials better than we've been doing so far, we have other problems.
- OK, repurpose a stadium.
- Or with the money we'd save on all the previous proposals, build something especially suited like the Imperial Senate Chamber from Star Wars Episode I - The Phantom Menace.[50]
- ***Too many things have been kept secret from us, dang it.***

Conclusion

*"If my people, which are called by my name, shall humble themselves, and pray, and seek my face, and turn from their wicked ways; then will I hear from heaven, and will forgive their sin, and will heal their land." — **2 Chronicles 7:14, KJV***

From even a secular perspective, 2 Chronicles 7:14 describes the inseparable connection between the individual, and the society we collectively create. So, ***thank you!*** It's only the most curious, motivated minds that find books like this. Thank you for your willingness to look past the numbing noise and partisan chest-pounding all around us, to at least consider an alternative cultural paradigm. Perhaps you can find courage in that it never takes more than a minority to direct societies. Summarizing all the previous chapters, there are four key points:

5. Our government, and its now-enormous superstructure, is corrupt. The people on the ballot are not running the world. It's puppet masters we unwittingly empower as the "Two Party System."
6. Those people telling us what we can do, can't do and must do, have no authority to do that. Written constitutions are the only authority for any power over us. As our politicians violate their constitutional oaths, they nullify all legitimate authority. The people pulling our politicians' strings never had any authority at all.
7. Whatever power any have over us is power we give them, and we can withdraw that power whenever we choose. …And by any means that we choose.
8. In every way, We the People *are*, and *must be*, our nation's government.

I hope you agree that our existing constitution's design, flaws notwithstanding, is the best compromise, and best social compact that our species has ever made law. And it's ours already. We need only demand it with our daily actions, and choices on Election Day. Abraham Lincoln became President with less than 40% in a four-way race. Eighteen other POTUS races have been won without a majority. Hundreds of "third-party" and independent politicians are already in office today. Perhaps a peaceful revolution has already begun.

But if you have a better idea…let's talk. Something has to change here. And it's about to, very significantly, very soon. One way, or another.

About the author

Andrew Horning worked in cardiodiagnostic technology, public health, cardiac research, clinical, education and industry roles since 1977. However, much of what was earned in professional endeavors had been blown on thirty years of quixotic political campaigns, protests, activism and lawsuits against a two-headed political monster. His political candidacies for Indiana Governor, US Senate and House of Representatives have been mostly under the Libertarian Party banner. But in 2004 Horning won the GOP primary election against the party's slate for US House of Representatives, and it's likely that he also won the general election (if counting only living voters). – Horning's campaign team documented significant election fraud using simple retrospective analysis of abandoned homes and voting records that year, which won some notice of the district's shenanigans from out-of-state newspapers such as The Wall Street Journal and Chicago Tribune.

A tax protest led by Horning on July 4, 2007, also earned national media, and has been credited with both a turnover of the Indianapolis city government, and a kick start to the "Tea Party Movement."

Horning is a former weekly columnist for Indiana's biggest daily newspaper, and an Adjunct Scholar with the Indiana Policy Review Foundation.

He's also a passionate advocate for *asimina triloba*, the "Indiana Banana," or American Pawpaw.

He is most happy when ensconced in his life of family and never-ending projects on a small farm in middle-of-nowhere Freedom, Indiana. Two fishable creeks, an occasionally stocked pond, and of course woods filled with pawpaws over comfortably hilly terrain, make it a hillbilly paradise from which he hopes to stimulate a Peaceful Revolution of Liberty and Justice…for *All*. At long last.